The Life Legacy Gift:

Creating a Lasting Legacy Whilst Living a Fulfilled Life

"Legacy. What is a legacy? It's planting seeds in a garden you never get to see."

Lin-Manuel Miranda, playwright

Contents

Foreword

I was fortunate that I didn't experience loss until I was 12. The grief I must have felt is not something engrained in my memory, but the impact of this death has left a lasting impact on my life.

Like my father and his father before him, I grew up in a farming family. 'G.E. Reading and Sons', our family business, was founded by my grandad, Gerald Reading, in 1939. As Britain entered into war, my grandad ventured into his own unknown territory. The land where my grandad envisioned his farm to be situation the Brundenell Estate in Deene, but his family pleaded with him not to rent here, due to its proximity to the Corby Steel Works. They feared the farm would become a target for Nazi bombings; a prophecy that would come true before the war ended.

My grandad was an exceptionally generous, gentle, kind, and evidently brave man, who relished any opportunity to spoil his grandchildren. I have incredibly fond memories of him, and I am eternally proud of the legacy he left behind. He died when I was 12.

In a fairly standard Will, he left most of his assets to Grandma, my dad and my uncles, who had all taken over running the family farm together. He also left a relatively small lump sum directly to each grandchild. Dad, being sensible with money, invested wisely and ensured that when the time was right, it could be used to help my sister and I make a start in life. It wasn't until I was 21 that this financial legacy really made a difference.

Like a good farmer's son, I studied agriculture at Newcastle University and returned to the farm at the end of my degree. However, 6 months into the farming life, I realised that it was not the life for me. I didn't love farming, and it's a hard slog if your heart isn't in it; however, I didn't know what else to do.

I discussed this with Mum and Dad, and we agreed that some time spent travelling was what I needed to clear my head and to work out a plan for the next few years. The money Grandad had put aside was my ticket to explore new worlds, meet new people and learn about other cultures. I vehemently believe that I learned more in 6 months of travelling than I did in 3 years at university.

In my book 'Entrepreneurial Happiness', I tell the story of my travels, and how I met my uncle, Bill, in Perth, Australia. Bill was the man who lit the fires in my entrepreneurial genes, which my dad had been cultivating both consciously and subconsciously throughout my whole life. Sometimes you can't see the wood for the trees, and Bill helped me to see that running my own business didn't necessarily have to mean running a farm.

To cut a very long story short, I fell into Financial Services by mistake upon my return to the UK, when I decided to move to London. Despite wanting to help people manage their money, I really didn't like the unscrupulous way the industry operated, so I set up my own firm, Efficient Portfolio, in 2006. The rest, as they say, is history. Success didn't come overnight, but as I write, Efficient Portfolio have recently been crowned as the top financial planning firm in the Midlands, are one of the few Chartered firms in the UK, and are regularly rated as one of the top UK firms by The Sunday Telegraph, Sunday Times and top industry magazines. We've also just been awarded our British Standards Kite Mark, so it hasn't gone too badly!

Had I not gone travelling I wouldn't have had the courage to move to London or to venture into my own unknown territory. Travelling enabled me to meet some contacts in London, who helped to get my career off the ground, but it also gave me the opportunity to meet my late uncle, who showed me how running your own business can give you an amazing life on your terms.

I was extremely fortunate to be left a legacy by my grandad, as it allowed me to go off and see the world when I most needed to. However, I am sure that the entrepreneurial spirit and values that I witnessed from him, and my family were equally as important. Maybe it's almost fate, based on where I ended up professionally, that I saw first-hand the benefits of investing your money wisely!

Leaving a legacy isn't just about the money you leave behind though; it is about the lessons, values and memories you pass on to others. The experiences and opportunities these create are what really changes the lives of the people you care most about.

Chapter 1: The Life Legacy Gift Approach

We spend our lives working hard, developing our skills, learning life's lessons, and building our wealth. In my experience we do all of those things for two real reasons: firstly, to give ourselves the best life we can; and secondly, to also create a better life for the people we care most about. At Efficient Portfolio, our overriding ethos is that we want to 'help people create a better future through inspirational financial planning', and by that we mean for our clients, our team and our industry. I am sure you are no different; you want to create a better future for yourself, your family and perhaps also your community or industry too.

The aim of this book is to help you and us create a better future. If we can help you create a better legacy for your family, and an enriching life for yourself, then we are achieving our ultimate aim. If you can do it, you are creating a better future for the people you care most about, including yourself.

If you are already a client of Efficient Portfolio, we already take care of many of the essential aspects of your finances, so you are on the right track; however, there are many facets to your overall happiness and the legacy you leave behind that we cannot help you with. Therefore, one of the functions of this book is also to help you better organise your estate so that, when the worst happens, the people left behind are well equipped to deal with it, but also so that your hard work is not undone by future generations.

When considering what to call this book, I wondered whether the title should be 'Death: A User's Guide'. It wouldn't have been the cheeriest title on the bookshelf, but it would have been a fair description of what is all about. However, I realised that this book isn't actually about death; it's about making the most of life, both now and for generations to come. Life only has context and meaning because of death.

This book is a way of inspiring you, so that you can consider how to give your life the meaning it deserves, as well as ensuring that you live on beyond your death. It is about leaving a legacy: a gift to those people you care most about. Hence, 'The Life Legacy Gift' was born. The name won't leap off the shelf as well as the working title, but better portrays the benefit I hope you'll get from reading it.

This book is broken into three sections to make it easier to digest. I encourage you to read all sections, even if you want to prioritise one particular aspect. It can be easy to assume that the legacy we leave is all about the money, but actually it is the less tangible elements of life that will survive from one generation to the next. Ultimately, money will be spent on clearing mortgages, buying cars and treating your loved ones to holidays, so it's a source that can bring comfort and short-lived happiness, and it may well get forgotten in the generations to come. Fundamentally, it is the values, principles and memories that you leave behind that will make a lasting impact, but sadly these can be easily lost forever. That's why this book is about creating a 'Life Legacy Gift', so that you can ensure that your unique family heritage is passed down indefinitely and enjoyed in the here and now.

Section 1: Life

The first section of this book will take care of the essentials, such as the non-financial documents and domestic admin that have built up during your life. This section is about how you can make life easier for your surviving loved ones and will prepare them for what to expect in the first couple of weeks following your departure from this Earth. Unless you have experienced the loss of a close family member, there can be a lot of critical things to plan for and take into account, which can be easily overlooked. Without prior planning, what is already a devastating time for the people who love you, is compounded by the distress of trying to track down key information.

One of the key features of section 1 is 'The Life F.I.L.E': a 4-step process to help ensure there is a plan for the practical things like passwords, alarm codes or keys, plus who needs to know, and when and how. We will also look at what people need to make the probate process as painless, efficient and cost effective as possible.

Section 2: Legacy

The second section is about the legacy you create and leave, and concentrates on your finances. If you don't properly organise this part, all the hard work you've put in to secure a legacy can be decimated in a frighteningly short space of time, or even worse, you could run out during your lifetime. This section includes the 'The Don't W.A.I.T. Protection Plan' and gives you a 4-step guide on how you can maximise the legacy you leave, minimise tax and ensure your wealth passes down the bloodline for generations to come.

Section 3: Gift

The final section is about the gift you can leave to the people you care most about. Whether that is your family, friends, community, charity or industry, this section will show you how you can best pass on your memories, life lessons and the values you have created during your lifetime. If you miss this element, all this knowledge, wisdom and wealth of experiences will be lost forever, and generations to come will have to learn by making the same mistakes as you. This section also includes the 'The P.A.S.T. Gift', which helps you to ensure that your legacy outlives the money you leave behind, just like what my grandad gifted me.

In a digitally driven world, I wanted to give you the opportunity to create your Legacy Life Gift in whatever format works best for you. If I am honest, probably both digitally and physically is best in this instance. So, in order for you to be able to create this digitally, you will need to download 'The Legacy Life Gift Planner' from www.efficientportfolio.co.uk/life-legacy-gift. That way, as you go through the book, or afterwards if you prefer, you can build your own personalised version.

The first attempt at completing this document probably won't be the final version, as this resource will evolve. Something is always better than nothing, but I encourage you to complete it fully over time. It is vital this is stored securely, as it will contain a huge amount of your personal information and needs to be safeguarded against risks such as fire, physical and digital theft, or the possibility of your device breaking. If you are a client, I would suggest you keep it in your Client Portal, as this is a highly secure online store, where the information can be easily retrieved. If you want us to help you access your portal, please just get in touch. All that said though, a physical copy, again safely stored, is a good plan too, so The Legacy Life Gift Planner can easily be printed out, and elements updated as needed.

I hope you enjoy the journey of creating your very own Life Legacy Gift. The details you'll document are a culmination of your life's work and achievements, so I believe that it is also a very rewarding experience. Enjoy the journey and remember that 'progress not perfection' is the key here. What you do will make a huge impact on the people you care most about, including some people you may never meet, so enjoy the ride and be creative! After all, this is your life, and you have the power for it to be remembered and enjoyed in any way you want.

Section 1:

The Life F.I.L.E.

F   Family Life

I   Immediate Life

L   Legal Life

E   Everyday Life

"Legacy is not leaving something for people. It's leaving something in people."

Peter Strople, Business Strategist

Chapter 2: Immediate Life

The First 14 Days

The subject of death is always an incredibly delicate topic, and one that none of us relish considering. Ultimately, death is a very sad and devastating part of all of our lives, but it is also an inescapable eventuality.

There are of course different types of deaths: ones that happen out of the blue, and others that are more expected. We all hear about 'good deaths' and 'bad deaths'. I will not expand on the latter of these, but in terms of a 'good death', I know that many of us share the idyll of death coming to us in our sleep at a ripe old age, after having lived a full and happy life. But it is not just the physical act of passing that can be considered 'good' or 'bad': There are also good and bad deaths from a legacy point of view too. Some deaths can cause increased devastation because of the additional strain put on the family to sort out an unintentional mess, or because so much of importance was lost. Anything we can do to minimise that pain and maximise that legacy, or those cherished memories, will prove to be a blessing further down the road.

When people think of preparing for death, they think about writing a Will. That is of course sensible, and we will come onto that; however, what normally happens is that the Will is not even read until after the funeral. There is an awful lot that needs to happen before that stage.

Exercise 1

I would like to pose a rather morbid, but crucial question: If you had died an hour ago, what would have happened? And what would you have wanted to happen?

You can think about this from a number of perspectives:

How do your loved ones find out?

Who will help those dependent on you?

What is unfinished, and how will that affect others?

Do people know where your information and documents are?

Who can access the house / safe?

Who knows your funeral wishes? Who should know?

You should also use **The Life Legacy Planner** to collate the following information about your key people:

> ➢ Their name
> ➢ Your relationship with them
> ➢ Their address
> ➢ Their telephone numbers
> ➢ Their email address

In order to prepare for the worst, you need to come up with a plan. The first stage of that plan should look at how the news of your passing will be communicated. I suggest you write out a plan for who needs to know about your death, and when and how these people should be told. Think about who is the best person to tell your loved ones the sad news. Aside from family and close friends, also think about your wider friendship groups, your community, any societies, or groups you are part of, and your place of work. The best way to document this is in **The Life Legacy Planner**.

Day of Death

Whilst this section won't affect you after your own passing, it is useful to know what to expect in case someone who you care about has passed away. It is also valuable to pass this information onto those who will be around after your passing. In terms of the practicalities surrounding death, it can be hard to know what to do on the day someone passes away. In truth, the individual situation will dictate what you should do.

Within a couple of hours of dying, unless special arrangements have been made (for example on religious grounds), most of us will be taken to a funeral home or Chapel of Rest. However, before the deceased can be put into the care of the undertakers, a doctor must confirm the death and present written confirmation.

1. If someone dies in hospital, a hospice or a care home, the staff will arrange for a doctor to confirm the death.
2. If you unexpectedly find your loved one, and they have passed away, call 999 and the attending doctor or paramedic team will arrange for the death to be confirmed.
3. If your loved one is receiving palliative care at home, you are likely to be advised to call 111, as the death is expected. The doctor confirming the death will notify any NHS District Nurses/care teams, who will collect any equipment and ensure that the room where the deceased passed is cleaned down. If you are using private care providers, you will need to contact them directly.

Once the doctor has confirmed death, and if no further tests are required, you can then contact the funeral home of your choice. They will collect the deceased and take them to the Chapel of

Rest. They will then be in touch for you to make arrangements for the funeral. If the death is unexpected, or suspicious, the deceased will be taken to a coroner. Once released, the funeral home can step in.

Access

On the day of your passing, it may be necessary for someone to access your home and some of your information. Doing what I do, I like to think my family should be fairly well organised with regards to their planning, so when discussing the points in this book with my mum and dad recently, I was somewhat shocked to hear that they have a safe. Not only did I not know how to access this, but I also didn't even know it existed or where it was!

Had I not had this conversation with them, I would have certainly struggled to access some of their most important documents and possessions. Talking to them also brought to light several other questions: who has the keys to their house? Who has the alarm code? Where are the keys for internal doors, or out-buildings? These are important questions for everyone, but if you live alone, these are crucial points to consider.

The moral of the story is to ensure that at least one person who you trust has a way of accessing your home, and of course your safe or filing cabinets. Again, this can be documented in your **Life Legacy Planner.**

ICE

On the day you die, you may of course not be at home or with one of your loved ones. If this were to happen, how would your family be informed? One of the most practical ways to deal with any immediate difficulties is to have emergency contact details in your mobile phone. Nowadays most phones have emergency contact information that can be accessed without the passcode, but ensure this is correctly set, or that your passcode is clearly communicated or documented. If you have the emergency function on your phone, make sure the details are completed correctly. If not, put a contact into your phone called ICE (In-Case of Emergency) so that the emergency services can contact the right person if they need to. Having an emergency contact is not just useful in the event of your death, it is also a sensible step to take in case you have an accident, or even simply lose your phone!

The Next 2-5 Days

A couple of days after passing, ideally the next step is for the family is to register the death, and to do this you will need a Medical Certificate of Cause of Death (MCCD) and the deceased's NHS card/number. To register a death, you ordinarily need to take the written confirmation you received from the doctor on the day of death to the deceased's GP. They will then issue you with a MCCD, which needs to be presented to the Registrar. You can normally obtain this within 48 hours.

A death should generally be registered within 5 days', but registration can be delayed for another 9 days if the Registrar is told that a medical certificate has been issued but you have not been able to secure an appointment. If the death has been reported to the coroner, you cannot register it until the coroner's investigations are concluded.

You will need to book an appointment to register the death. The Registrar will tell you what documents you need to take with you, but this will typically include the deceased's Birth or Marriage Certificate, proof of ID and the MCCD Form. The Registrar will know that you need to register the death within 5 days, so will make you a priority.

The Registrar will issue two documents: a Certificate for Burial and an Application for Cremation. This is often known as the green certificate or form. It gives permission for the body to be buried or for an application for cremation to be made, and you should give this to the Funeral Director.

The Registrar will also provide you with some useful guidance about what your local authority can do to help in terms of notifying the appropriate Governmental institutions (e.g., DVLA, local council) of the death, which is done by an automated system.

A similar system, called the Death Notification Service (www.deathnotificationservice.co.uk) can be used to notify most large banks, building societies and insurers of the death, so it's a useful resource to save you time and hassle at this difficult time. You will need account details for this service.

Once you have received the Green Form from the Registrar, you will need to present this to the Funeral Director. Before we move onto the funeral though, it's worth noting that your GP can be a great source of help for people who are dealing with death. They can help with returning any specialist equipment, provide guidance on what to do with surplus medication, facilitate and recommend support groups, and help with cancelling prescriptions or appointments.

Funeral Wishes

As I mentioned, putting your funeral wishes in a Will is often pointless as the Will is usually read after the event. If you want your funeral to be actioned in a certain way, you need to let the funeral organisers know in advance.

My best friend from university was a dairy farmer from Cornwall called Rob. A larger-than-life guy who led me astray in my formative years! We had so much in common, but one key differentiator was his love of the farm. He was passionate about his herd and breeding the best milking cows possible. It made me laugh that instead of bringing a girlfriend to my 21st birthday party, he brought a cow that he was transporting to market.

After University, Rob established himself as a successful entrepreneur, and just as a few of his ventures were taking shape and the jigsaw pieces of his personal life were fitting nicely together, he was killed in a light aircraft crash in his 30th year. Having been his Best Man, I was asked to read a eulogy at his funeral, something that I found incredibly difficult to do.

Rob had mentioned in passing at his granny's funeral that he didn't like the misery of an all-black attire affair, so we were asked by the family to wear a spectrum of colours, not just the standard black and white. I must confess that I partially ignored this, as I wanted to pay homage to his beloved Newcastle United (nicknamed 'The Magpies' because of the colours of their kit)- I know he approved. As we left the church that day, we did so to the sound of Fat Les' football anthem 'Vindaloo'. Had his family not known him so well as to make that call, I am not sure I'd have been brave enough to suggest that as his farewell song, for fear of what others might think. You see, if you know what someone wants, you are free to make those calls without worry or fear of being judged. Because we knew him so well, we could play his favourite song and make a playful nod to his football team.

So, did Rob really want a more colourful funeral? Yes, because by chance he happened to mention it and his mum remembered. Did he want Vindaloo blasting out of the church? Knowing Rob, I dare say it would have made him smile. Would he have wanted something else? We have no idea, because, at the age of 30, he hadn't thought about it.

If you want to make things easier for your loved ones at a desperately painful point in their lives, now is the time to plan what you would actually like. Here are some more questions to prompt your thoughts:

Do you want to be buried, cremated, or something else?

What do you want to happen at your funeral?

Where do you want the service?

What hymns/non-religious songs would you like sung or played?

Do you want a religious, non-religious or hybrid service?

Do you want an obituary in your local newspaper?

What readings would you like?

Who would you like to speak?

What music do you want played?

How do you want people to dress?

What flowers, photos or items do you want displayed?

Do you want a wake? If so, where?

Where do you want your ashes scattered or your burial to be?

If you do put some thought into this, you'll make the proceedings far less painful to organise, and the people you leave behind will know they gave you the send-off you wanted.

The important thing here is to get the answers to these questions written down, and then to let the people around you know where they can find them. You can of course use **The Life Legacy Planner** for that purpose, so if you've not done so already, download it now and start to get some of these questions   answered.

Chapter 3: Family Life

I mentioned earlier that there can be such a thing as a 'good death' and a 'bad death'; if you don't believe me I suggest you read '33 Meditations on Death: Notes from the Wrong End of Medicine' by NHS consultant in geriatric and stroke medicine, David Jarrett. It is a darkly humorous book, and I promise you it will give you a different perspective on death.

I am writing this book in 'Lockdown Part 3'. Please tell me it is only a trilogy, and this is the final chapter! But humour aside, the context of my writing is important, because it's the time when the nation is mourning the loss of Captain Sir Tom Moore, who at the age of 100 fell victim to COVID-19.

Captain Sir Tom achieved a huge amount during his life, and in his final chapter, his 100th year, he raised nearly £33m for the NHS, had a number 1 single and was knighted by Her Majesty The Queen. That's a pretty amazing swan song isn't it!

So, are we right to mourn his sad passing from COVID-19, the virus he raised so much money to fight? Yes of course. But are we right to call it a 'good death'? I think so. It was relatively quick, he was with his family, and he was over 100. That to me, and to Jarrett, would be described as a 'good death'.

My nanna, on the other hand, definitely had a 'bad death'. She was the heart and soul of our family and of the Northamptonshire farming community; her ability to force feed you sausage rolls and sweet treats was second to none! During my many days staying with her and 'Gramp' in Stanwick, there would be a constant stream of visitors from the village, the farm and from the wider local community popping in for a cup of tea, some cake or even a tongue sandwich. Not sure I miss that last one!

Sadly, all those delicious foods caught up with her, and one day, out of the blue, she had a stroke. Now a good death would probably have been for her to pass right there and then. But she didn't. She lost most of the use of her left side, her speech, and her ability to do any of the things she loved. She spent some time in hospital, then lived with us for quite a while, and spent her last years in a care home. She never regained her speech, and very little movement, and she lived on like this for another 5 years after having had that stroke.

I'll never forget Rob coming to stay, perhaps when he bought the cow over for my 21st. During dinner one night, Nanna spent the entire meal starring at Rob's eyebrow piercing. I would have loved to hear what she would have said had she been able, but of course she couldn't. During those 5 years she struggled to move, to communicate and to remember the people who loved her most. In my mind, the person Nanna was died when she had that stroke; she just remained with us physically for a few more years. If she'd been one of the animals on her farm, she'd have had it put down out of kindness.

The death that my nanna experienced is, in my mind, a bad death, and sadly most of us know other examples of these. Those last 5 years must have been torture for her, having had such a fun filled, family and friend orientated 80 years prior.

In quite a few situations, many of us won't have much control over the type of death that lies ahead for us, however, Jarrett's advice in '33 Meditations on Death' is to document how you want the end of your life to look. Do you want to go into care? Would you want certain treatments to prolong your life? Where would you want to spend your final days? These are very emotive questions but will help your loved ones, and potentially provide you with the best possible outcome for your final days and weeks on Earth.

What kind of medical treatment do you, or don't you, want to have?

Where would you prefer to be when you die?

Who do you want to be with when you die?

Who do you want to designate to make medical decisions on your behalf when you are unable to make them yourself?

Are you willing or unwilling to donate your organs or tissues?

Where is your donor card? (If you don't have one it's quick and easy to register on the NHS Organ Donation website: www.organdonation.nhs.uk)

There is another question here that may need to be considered, and that is regarding resuscitation. It is an incredibly difficult choice to make and is usually only posed to those facing terminal illnesses. If you do fall into this category, this decision will need to be made in conjunction with your GP and palliative care team, as specific documentation must be drawn up.

In order for people to act on your behalf you'll need a Lasting Power of Attorney, more on that later, but documenting what you do and don't want to happen will help them make the right decisions when you can't. You can complete these questions in **The Life Legacy Planner** as a good starting point, so the people who you love can make the best decisions possible in line with your wishes.

Once you've collated your thoughts, the next step may also be to create a Living Will or an Advance Decision. This is a legally binding document that lets you say if you don't want certain types of medical treatment in certain situations, especially if you lose capacity in the future. For example, you may want to refuse to receive a blood transfusion if it's against your religion. Advance Decisions are free to make, and you don't need to go via a solicitor; however, you do need to be over 18, and have mental capacity when you make it, for it to be valid.

While Advance Decisions are legally binding, and are only about treatments you want to refuse, if you want to ensure others know about how you want to be treated towards the end of life, you can make an 'Advance Statement'. This document lets you state anything you think others should know, so that they can best care for you in the future, especially if you lose the capacity to communicate. To make an Advance Statement, write down your wishes, sign it and keep it somewhere safe, like with **The Life Legacy Planner.** Again, ensure your loved ones know where it's kept. You can also ask your doctor to keep a copy in your medical notes. See the NHS website www.nhs.uk/conditions/end-of-life-care/advance-statement for more information.

Key Information

The people who are left behind will need access to a huge amount of information from your life to be able to register your death, to be able to cancel anything that will no longer be needed, and to be able to get probate granted. I mentioned earlier that to register a death you need the deceased's NHS card or number. I don't know about you, but as I write this, I have no idea where my NHS card is. Fortunately, I do keep a copy of my NHS number securely with all my passwords, but I don't know the NHS numbers of my family.

Finding out this information while you are here is a whole lot easier than someone else having to find it out after you have gone, so it will make everyone's lives easier if you have all your key information documented in one place, such as in **The Life Legacy Planner**.

Here is a list of key information you will need. Please note that not all details will be relevant to everyone:

> ➤ Your full legal name
> ➤ Alternative name(s)
> ➤ Address
> ➤ Telephone numbers
> ➤ Email address
> ➤ Nation Insurance number
> ➤ Driving License number
> ➤ Passport number
> ➤ Place of birth
> ➤ Blood type
> ➤ Birth Certificate location
> ➤ Marriage Certificate location
> ➤ Marital status
> ➤ Spouse or partner's name
> ➤ Spouse or partner's address
> ➤ Spouse or partner's telephone numbers
> ➤ Spouse or partner's email address

Repeat the last 4 points above for any children, grandchildren, siblings, parents, financial dependants, or former spouses you may have. If your children have guardians, include their details too.

> ➤ Decree Absolute location (if applicable)
> ➤ Mother's place of birth
> ➤ Father's place of birth
> ➤ Your occupation and company name
> ➤ Your work email, address and telephone number
> ➤ Details of any religious organisations you belong to

- Former Military/Police/Fire/NHS employment details, including your public sector pension number
- Your Financial Planner's name, address, email, and telephone number
- Your Accountant's name, address, email, and telephone number
- Your Insurance Broker's name, address, email, and telephone number
- Your Solicitor's name, address, email, and telephone number
- Your Investment Manager's name, address, email, and telephone number
- Any other professional adviser's name, address, email, and telephone number
- Your Health Insurance provider's name, address, email, and telephone number
- Your clergy person's name, address, email, and telephone number
- Your GP's name, address, email, and telephone number
- Your specialist's name, address, email, and telephone number
- Your NHS number and card location
- Your Donor Card number and location
- Details of any existing medical conditions
- Details of any medication you are prescribed and their location
- Details of any allergies you may have
- Your preferred hospital name, address, and contact details

It's quite a list, isn't it? If you think it is difficult trying to get all this information together now, imagine what it would be like for your nearest and dearest during the grieving process! That is why it is so important to do it now. You just never know when it all will be needed.

One thing you will see on the list is your donor card. Your decision here can be life changing for someone else, so it is important that if you're a UK resident and you're willing, you do actively indicate that you are happy to donate your organs after your passing.

Countries like Portugal, Poland, France and Austria have almost 100% of their drivers agreeing to donate their organs. In contrast to this, countries like the UK (17%), Netherlands (28%), Denmark (4%) and Germany (12%) have far lower donor registrations. The reason the first group of countries has such a high sign-up rate is simple: when they complete the forms to register their driving licence, they have to tick a box if they want to opt out of donating their organs. Conversely, all the countries in the second group have to opt in to organ donation.

In this case, the format of a form is the difference between saving thousands of lives and not. Make sure you make the right choice for you, not the person who designed the form!

The Finances

If there is going to be a family dispute after your passing, chances are that it will be over money; therefore, if you want to keep your family on speaking terms, it is vital the financial side of things is clear. It is also crucial that those administering your estate can get access to all the financial information as quickly and as easily as possible, so that the cost and speed of probate can be kept to a minimum.

As a client of Efficient Portfolio, you'll find your Client Portal is an incredibly powerful resource in this department. The problem with any list is remembering to update it. Your Client Portal will list most, if not all, of your investments, provide the relevant paperwork for them, and even provide a live and up-to-date valuation. You can even use it to store The Life Legacy

Planner. You might also want to keep a folder somewhere in the house that contains a printed-out version of The Life Legacy Planner and your latest Quarterly Investment Statement or your Annual Review Pack. That way there is always a list of your assets to hand. Of course, if you aren't a client of Efficient Portfolio, you may not have these, so it is prudent to create and regularly update your own records, both digitally and in paper format.

The Assets List

Making your money work hard for you means that you, or the people who you care about, don't need to work as hard themselves. If you are a client of Efficient Portfolio, I'd imagine that you only hold cash as an emergency fund, and also for any planned and upcoming expenditures. Other than that, the rest of your money should be getting you the best returns possible for a level of risk you are comfortable with and be held in a properly diversified portfolio. If this is the case, for the reasons I've already listed, you've already made your life and the lives of your loved ones much easier. That said, there may be certain types of assets we don't manage for you, so it's important to also document these details of these, which can be done using **The Asset List**. This will make the lives of your Executor's so much easier.

As a note here, if cash has started to build up again for you, or there are any assets that you'd like to be reviewed, speak to your Financial Planner about optimising your money.

The Asset List
BANK SND BUILDING SOCIETY ACCOUNTS

- ➢ Name of account
- ➢ Owner(s) of account
- ➢ Bank or Building Society name

- ➢ Account number and sort code
- ➢ Approximate balance

SAVINGS ACCOUNTS

- ➢ Name of account
- ➢ Owner(S) of account
- ➢ Bank or institution name
- ➢ Account number and sort code
- ➢ Approximate balance

INVESTMENTS

- ➢ Name of account
- ➢ Owner(S) of account
- ➢ Type of investment
- ➢ Institution where the investment is held
- ➢ Manager of account
- ➢ Account number
- ➢ Approximate balance

PENSIONS

- ➢ Name of account
- ➢ Owner(S) of account
- ➢ Type of pension
- ➢ Institution where the pension is held
- ➢ Manager of account
- ➢ Account number
- ➢ Approximate balance

SHARES

- ➢ Name of owner(s)
- ➢ Company that provides the shares and their contact details
- ➢ Number of shares held
- ➢ Account number

- ➢ Approximate value
- ➢ Manager of shares

PROPERTY

- ➢ Name and address of property
- ➢ Owner(s)
- ➢ Related mortgage details
- ➢ Status of property (i.e., let to tenants, holiday let or main residence)
- ➢ Company who manages the property (e.g., letting agent)
- ➢ Approximate value
- ➢ Freehold or leasehold

If, for some reason, you aren't a client of ours, you may have assets scattered more widely. If that is the case, you can make your Beneficiaries' lives easier by completing **The Asset List**, but you may also find it helpful to speak to us about optimising your finances, so that they deliver a consistent return, both whilst you are alive and afterwards. Sadly, when my nanna died, she left her children some shares in Enron. By the time the probate process was complete they had gone from a significant holding to being worthless. Had her money been invested in a diversified portfolio, my relatives would have inherited significantly more than they did.

Insurance

Insurance is rarely seen as the most exciting or enjoyable way to spend your money, but it can be the difference between disaster and diversion. I'll cover more about how to use insurance to improve your legacy in the next section, however for now I want to deal with making sure that the people who you support do not suffer financially after your demise.

The type of insurance you'll need depends on your stage in your life. If you have a young family that is dependent on your income, it is probably the most important thing you can spend your money on; whereas if you are retired, with sufficient money put aside for both you and your spouse to live a long life, your needs will be very different. I don't want to go into much detail here, because it is difficult to be generic in such a wide-ranging set of scenarios. That said, there are some principles that are important to consider. Ultimately, the best thing you can do here is to seek advice from an Independent Financial Planner like Efficient Portfolio.

The most expensive insurance you'll ever pay for is the one that doesn't pay out, so make sure you have the essentials covered through policies that are underwritten in the correct way. Policies underwritten at the point of claim, like PPI and Accident and Sickness Policies, are a waste of money for most people. Only finding out if you are eligible to claim at the time when you need it most is useless. Where possible, only get policies that are underwritten at the point of application, so the likelihood of them covering you when you need them is far higher.

Make sure your home insurance is held in joint names. A deceased person cannot hold an insurance policy, so if you spouse remains in the house but isn't on the policy, they could find that they have no cover for a period of time, and of course be unaware of this problem. To offset this risk, your Will needs to include an insurance clause that allows your Executor to take over your insurance. If we have facilitated your Will, it will include this clause, but if we haven't, please do check. The other thing to be aware of with home insurance is that most policies only allow the house to be vacant for 30 days, so if this would affect you, because you live on your own for example, consider that there may be no insurance just 1 month after your passing.

It worries me that more families insure their mobile phones than their family's financial future, or even their own. It is vital that you consider making sure the people you leave behind are sufficiently looked after from a financial point of view. I always think about this in really simple terms with the following questions:

How much income would you and your dependants need if you were sick?
(This is to pay bills, put food on the table, pay for education and holidays too)

How much income would your dependants need if you died?
(This is also to pay bills, put food on the table, pay for education and holidays too)

How much capital would you and your dependants need if you were sick?
(This is often to adapt the house, for treatment or recovery)

How much capital would your dependants need if you were to die?
(This is to clear debt, live off, purchase property etc.)

Once you've worked out the answers to these questions, and your Financial Planner can help you with that too, you can start to formulate the right blend of insurances to ensure that if the unexpected happens, the people around you are cared for.

If you are already retired and skipping through this section with a smile, think again if you have children. One of the excuses I hear most often for families not having appropriate life cover or financial protection is that the 'Bank of Mum and Dad' would step in when needed. The question is, is that OK with you? I know you would help your children and grandchildren if you needed to, but wouldn't it be better to ensure they have the right cover in the first place? If you'd like us to help ensure they do, feel free to introduce them to us!

The Insurance Directory

As with your other finances, it makes sense to have a list of your insurance policies. **The Life Legacy Planner** can keep these in one centralised place for you.

For each insurance policy you have in place, you will need to make a note of:

- The company providing the insurance
- The type of insurance
- The policy owner
- The policy number
- The benefit amount
- Who manages the policy (for example, a Financial Planner)

Types of insurance may include:

- Home insurance
- Private medical insurance
- Life insurance
- Income protection
- Critical illness cover
- Family income benefit
- IHT protection
- Pet insurance
- Car insurance
- Building and contents insurance
- Appliance and gadget protection (including mobile phones)

> ➤ Travel insurance
> ➤ Business insurance (for example Key Person Insurance

Pass the Baton!

For many families, there is usually one person who is responsible for keeping track of the finances. Historically, this was the 'man of the house', but increasingly I am seeing this change, especially with younger families.

When someone you love dies it is a traumatic experience, but combine that with the worry of knowing little or nothing of the family finances, and the pain increases immeasurably. With some of my older-generation clients, I have heard about all sorts of situations, including one where the widow could not fill her car up with petrol simply because her husband had always taken care of that. If just one of you knows where everything is, perhaps even manages some of the investments, it is vital you start to pass the baton.

This factor alone is one of the main reasons we always try to include both parties in a relationship in our financial planning meetings, so that there is transparency and knowledge on both sides. One of our roles for older couples is to provide the reassurance that, were something unexpected to happen, that we can guide the less active member through this time and give them confidence that their money is still being looked after.

I'd suggest that you ideally start to pass the baton now, so that both of you know what is going on with your money and there is less worry. However, rest assured, we will also be here to help, to give you the peace of mind that things are being taken care of and to talk you through the planning that is in place.

One way to pass the baton, particularly to the next generation, is to give them an easily digestible book around the principles of money. That's why I wrote my book 'SMART Money: How to Create Financial Freedom'. If you want to download a free copy you can from www.efficientportfolio.co.uk/smart

The Liabilities List

Sadly, some of your liabilities don't die with you, so the administrators of your estate will need to know what they are. One thing to consider is how will these debts be cleared if you were to die. Is there sufficient capital there that isn't needed for income? If not, you might need insurance to cover that debt, so someone else doesn't lose out on their intended inheritance, because they have to use it to pay off your liabilities.

Another thing to consider is whether you want your children to inherit your properties. If you do, and there isn't sufficient cash to pay the Inheritance Tax, not only will this slow down the process of them inheriting their share, but it may also mean that they miss out on the opportunity to maximise the assets' value. Insurance can solve this problem, but more on that in the next section of the book.

In order to help those left behind have clarity over what debts may be outstanding, and to help get probate granted in a more timely fashion, complete **The Liabilities List** in **The Life Legacy Planner.** It is important to keep this document updated on a regular basis, so that it is as accurate as possible.

This list will include the following details for your mortgage, credit card(s), store cards, car loan and unsecured debts.

> ➢ Owner
> ➢ Type
> ➢ Account/reference number
> ➢ Approximate amount outstanding
> ➢ Any other information

Chapter 4: Everyday Life

There is so much about normal everyday life that needs sorting out after people pass away. It is possible to document this, not just as a way to make the lives of your loved ones easier, but also to make your life easier between now and then. Seize the opportunity to tidy things up and everyone will benefit.

Digital

In this day and age, so much of our life is based in the digital world: our photos, our accounts and our utilities. Having a good password system has never been more important, but keeping track of every unique combination for the abundance of websites and online tools we use is a nightmare, isn't it?

We've all had those moments when a website tells us we have one last attempt before they lock us out and cause us an admin headache. You stare at the screen willing yourself to recall which is your favourite pet, thinking "I can't believe I just picked one", with the dog looking up at you as if to say, "It better be me!"

It used to be simple: We had a special word that was our password for everything. We used it for every website we registered for and felt safe in the knowledge that our special word would never be uncovered. That is until websites started accusing it of being 'weak!' They started asking us to put in a capital letter, so, after some careful deliberation, we capitalised the first letter of our special word. Then they wanted a number, and we placed a well thought out '1' after our special word. But still this wasn't enough, and the next commandment was for a special character to be incorporated. Again, more deliberation led us to the cunning conclusion that an '!' after the '1' at the end of our capitalised special word would fool the most devious of fraudsters. I'd hazard a guess that at this point you are considering changing your password from 'Dogsname1!'.

Everyone has a different way of remembering their passwords. Personally, I have a password protected document, where all passwords and their associated websites are alphabetised. I pick different ones every 6 months or so to avoid too much duplication, or as and when websites demand that I change. The beauty of having a centralised document is that I just need to remember one password to see them all.

Some people use an App like Dashlane, Roboform or Google Password Manager; whereas others, like my wife Caryl, have a memory-based system, which appears to fail at least 50% of the time. Other people may also use the paper-based-treasure-hunt system, where they hide a post-it note somewhere close to the PC, which they can never find when it's most needed! On a serious note, some methods are evidently more effective and secure than others, but the real message here is that if we can't remember our own passwords, what chance do our loved ones have?

Giving someone you trust access to all of your digital information can certainly help after you have passed away, but one word of warning here: if your loved ones log in as you for certain sites they may well be in breach of the sites terms and conditions, and could even face legal action, especially if what they are doing is seen as fraud. For certain websites, especially online banking, they will also need the correct permissions, such as a Lasting Power of Attorney, to access your financial details, so tread carefully.

Ultimately, it is up to your loved ones whether they choose to access your accounts using your passwords, and it is not my recommendation that they break the law! However, that being said, I know I would rather be safe in the knowledge that the right people have access to the right accounts when they need to, rather than them having to correspond with loads of companies for weeks on end at an unbelievably traumatic time. Personally, I'd rather put the decision in their hands to handle the situation as they see fit.

Whichever system you use, you need to put in place the provisions to pass the passwords on, when the time is right. Whether you use it to store your one password that accesses the others elsewhere, or you use it to store all your passwords, **The Life Legacy Planner** is of course a good option, as long as it is password protected itself. At least that way you only have to pass on one password to your loved ones, and when the time is right, they'll have access to all the accounts they need.

It is worth pointing out here that standard email is not a secure form of communication. In the same way as people can steal your post, people can hack your email accounts and steal your information and identity. I'd say that you should never email a document like **The Life Legacy Planner** or anything else that contains your passwords. Even if it doesn't get intercepted at the time, a hacker can still find it in your sent items, so never trust unsecure email to send or receive important details like bank account numbers or passwords. You never know whether the information will fall into the wrong hands.

This list should include:

> ➢ The company name
> ➢ Account number
> ➢ Username
> ➢ Password

> ➢ PIN
> ➢ Other information

Before saving your passwords here it is important that you password protect this document. Instructions on how to do that can be found in the appendices. *Also share this password with your loved ones, but also insist that they too keep it secure.*

Utilities

Henry Elliston, one of the Chartered Financial Planners at Efficient Portfolio, recently told me the story of his father-in-law. Sadly, he died very suddenly in his sleep when he was 57. He lived in a large farmhouse in the countryside, with several acres of land, outhouses, and lawns that he regularly mowed with his state-of-the-art sit-on mower.

Ahead of the wake the grass needed cutting, but the keys for the lawnmower were nowhere to be seen. The house was searched high and low but to no avail. Two days before the funeral, Henry's mother-in-law had a dream in which her late husband appeared and directed her to a secret hiding place. Sure enough, the following morning she went down to the chest in the work-shed, and there at the back of the drawer were keys. Needless to say, the lawns were immaculate for the remembrance celebration.

It is a lovely story, and it is amazing what can come to us in our sleep, however it's not a great strategy to rely on, so it's much better to write down details such as these.

Another thing your Executors will need to know is who your utility providers are, particularly if you live on your own, so it is important that you also document them.

This list should include the following information for your providers of gas, electricity, water, telephone, broadband, mobile phone, TV services and music services:

- ➢ Company name
- ➢ Account number
- ➢ Username
- ➢ Password

Chattels

When you are drawing up a Will, it is often easier to refer to a Chattels List rather than listing specific items in the Will. That way, if you lose something, sell it or bin it, it doesn't require a Will update each time; instead, you can simply amend your Chattels List. This isn't about listing everything you own, but it is about listing your more valuable, sentimental, or meaningful items. Wouldn't it be a shame if that Ming Vase ended up on eBay courtesy of an unwitting benefactor? Or if your child couldn't track down that beloved trinket that reminds them of their childhood? This can also be a helpful process with regards to your home insurance, not just for identifying the most valuable items that should be listed on the policy, but also as it will help you more accurately estimate the amount needed for the policy sum assured.

I'd recommend making a list of all your most precious personal possessions, where you keep them, their approximate value and, if you have a preference as to who inherits it, who that is. This list should include:

- ➢ The name of the item
- ➢ The approximate value
- ➢ The location of the item
- ➢ The intended recipient

Remember to mention this in your Will, but more on that later.

Memberships

Some of our greatest experiences and friends come from the places where we are members. I am a member of Luffenham Heath Golf Club, which is an old, traditional Harry Colt designed course established in 1911. It is a wonderful club, and when a fellow member passes away, they notify us, fly the flag at half-mast, and occasionally organise something in their memory. In fact, having a generally older clientele, the joke is that they keep the flag at half mast, just in-case.

Asking your loved ones to notify your club or society that you have passed away allows your fellow members to remember you, to show their respect, and then notify others who would want to know but may not be known to your family. On a practical level, your loved ones may also need to cancel your membership fees! As such, it is best to keep a list of your memberships on **The Life Legacy Planner.**

This list should include:

> ➤ The name of the club or society
> ➤ Your membership number
> ➤ Contact details of the club or society
> ➤ Additional notes

Pets

Pets are part of your family, so whether they are the namesake of your password or not, they still need taking care of when you're gone. If you've ever been to Edinburgh, you may have been to visit the statue of a wee dog called Bobby- - the diminutive Skye Terrier who kept constant watch over his dead master's grave for fourteen years, such was his loyalty and devotion. But as lovely as the story is about the faithful 'Greyfriars Bobby', it would have been better that he had been taken care of and given a new home. I'm sure that is what you would want for your pets.

To ensure your pets are properly cared for, create a list that includes the following:

> Pet's name
> Pet's age
> Chip or ID number
> Vet's name and contact details
> Carer's name and contact details
> Instructions

Memorial

Finally, but certainly no less importantly, have you considered how people will remember their time with you when you are gone? Some people want a bench at a local beauty spot or their beloved golf club; others a tree planting somewhere special, and others something else entirely. The question is, what do you want? How can a little piece of you be brought back to life? I love the bench idea, as long as it is in the right spot and is used by those who want to remember, but here is a more exhaustive list with some other ideas for inspiration: (Links in the Bibliography section).

- Turn your ashes into jewellery.
- Install a bench in a memorable place.
- Get your ashes made into a sculpture or ornament, perhaps for the garden.
- Plant a memorial or butterfly garden.
- Put a plaque somewhere special.
- Create a memory book / capsule.

- Create a music playlist.
- Plant a tree with the ashes.
- Commission a piece of art.
- Purchase and name a star.
- Send a gift to people from your Will.
- Contribute your ashes to help with the creation of an eco-reef.
- Create a recipe book.
- Treat your loved ones to a trip of a lifetime.
- Make a teddy bear with your ashes.
- Have your ashes compressed into a vinyl record (yes, apparently this is something that people have done!)
- Create an Education Trust (more on that later).
- Keep and display your ashes in an ornamental urn.

Chapter 5: Legal Life

Whilst talking about the legalities surrounding your passing may not be the most riveting topic, it is certainly one of the most important.

One of the largest legal areas that will need to be considered after your death is probate, which can be a long and drawn-out process. Probate is a hefty subject on its own, so this isn't the place to delve too deeply into the intricacies surrounding this area of law; however, there a few important things that it is worth being aware of, so that you can make the process as painless and cost effective as possible. Ultimately, probate can become an incredibly expensive and painful experience for those involved; the worst example I've heard of was Marilyn Monroe's estate, where probate took 40 years to be finally settled! I'm sure yours won't be as painful or as drawn out as that, but it highlights the danger of not organising your affairs correctly when you are alive. Thankfully, if you follow the guidance in this book, probate should be a much smoother process for you!

The first stage of probate is for your loved ones to register your death. Once this has been done, the Will is read. It goes without saying then, that if you have a Will, which you frankly should, you need to make your Beneficiaries aware of this fact and notify them where the Will is stored and the details of the legal firm who will be conducting the reading. For this reading, it is important that the Beneficiaries meet the firm that put the Will in place. If they have their contact details, they will be able to ensure the reading takes place in a timely fashion.

In some cases, it may be your Financial Planner who has facilitated your Will, or indeed some other planning strategies surrounding your finances, so it's important that these details are also passed on. To use my firm, Efficient Portfolio, as an example, if one of our clients has passed away, we look to organise a meeting with the Beneficiaries in the first few weeks, so that we can explain areas such as the asset protection strategies and Trust planning that had been put in place. If you have a Trust Framework, it is vital that advice is sought from your Financial Planner and your solicitor, to ensure that the planning opportunities are maximised. When it comes to Trusts, not everyone understands the benefits of using these frameworks, so it would be a shame if all that hard work went to waste. In short, it's crucial that your Beneficiaries meet with whoever was managing your financial affairs, to ensure they make the best decisions possible with your money.

Once the contents of the Will and any associated financial planning strategies have been established, your family will need to identify which route they wish to take with probate, i.e., to do it themselves, or to use a law firm. The decision will generally be based upon the complexities of probate, but generally we would advocate professional guidance of some sort, so that nothing is missed. If you do go down this route, we would always encourage people to obtain a set fee quote for the work in advance, rather than some firms that will charge a percentage of the estate, which can amount to a significant sum. At Efficient Portfolio, we work with a range of solicitors, so if you are a client of ours, we can introduce your family to firms that can help with this process in a cost-effective way.

There is, of course, nothing wrong with undertaking the probate process yourself, however there are certain situations where it isn't appropriate to use the 'do-it-yourself' approach, some of which I've listed below:

- An insolvent estate;
- When a Beneficiary cannot be contacted;
- When there is likely to be a challenge to the Will;

- If a Beneficiary is under the age of 18 or cannot inherit at the age of 18;
- If there is a Life Interest;
- If the deceased owned a business or agricultural land;
- If the deceased is a Lloyds Name (this is very rare, as there are only around 250 of these individuals left who were Lloyds of London investors, known as 'Names');
- Where Trusts are a Beneficiary;
- Where there is Inheritance Tax payable, but insufficient cash to pay it;
- If a Beneficiary wants to vary their inheritance;
- Where overseas property is involved.

In these cases, it is easy to make a costly mistake, so it is worth being guided through the process by someone who is qualified and experienced.

Key Document List

WILL

➤ Location of original
➤ Key contact (e.g., Financial Planner or Will Writer)
➤ Copy location
➤ Executors' names, addresses, telephone numbers and email addresses
➤ Attorneys' names, addresses, telephone numbers and email addresses

LASTING POWER OR ATTORNEY: PROPERTY AND FINANCIAL AFFAIRS

➤ Location or original
➤ Key contact (e.g., Financial Planner or Solicitor)
➤ Copy location

> Attorneys' names, addresses, telephone numbers and email addresses

Similar details could also be documented for the following:

> Advance Decision / Advance Statement
> Driving License / Passport
> Car Registration Documents
> Cheque books
> Savings/Shares Certificates
> Mortgage papers and policy documents

The Probate Process

As touched upon in the previous section, after your funeral, whoever is administering your estate will need to contact the companies and people who have been dealing with your financial affairs, including your Will. The lists in **The Life Legacy Planner** will prove invaluable here.

But the companies to contact are not just your Financial Planner or accountant, so it is important to remind you here that you should also detail your bank accounts and policies on **The Life Legacy Planner** in case anything has been set up separately.

When a death is registered, a central note can be made upon request at the Registry that notifies almost all the different government departments (for example the DVLA and local council); however, all other institutions will need to be notified directly, and as quickly as possible. For some financial institutions, there is a centralised service that works in a similar way to the Government's Death Notification Service, whereby institutions where you held accounts will be notified. However, not all financial institutions subscribe to this service, so your loved ones will need to check that no companies have been missed.

In the case of banks, once your loved ones have notified them of your passing, your bank accounts will be frozen; however, until they notify companies such as your pension provider, income will continue to come in. In some cases, you would have been entitled to this money, so this should be placed in a 'probate account', which will make the completion of the estate's tax return easier as it demonstrates income that should be included in your estate. However, if companies are not notified immediately, income that you would not be entitled to could still find its way into your account, and this may then need to be paid back.

Once all providers and institutions have been notified, whoever is administering your estate will then need to gather up all of your assets. This can take a long time; however, it can be made immeasurably easier by the lists you will have completed **The Life Legacy Planner**.

Business Owners

If you own or run a business, there are some crucial decisions to make, and some important considerations to bear in mind. For example, the remaining directors could continue to run the company (if the company's Articles of Association allow this) and they can share out your responsibilities; however, other aspects aren't quite so easy, so there are a few things to consider.

If the deceased director is the only shareholder, and the company has been incorporated after 1st October 2006, under the Companies Act 2006 the model Articles of Association allow the personal representatives of the deceased officer to appoint a new director. For companies incorporated before this date, and companies that have not adopted the model articles, you should seek professional advice about your options, and these can be quite complex.

Key to the Business' Survival?

The next consideration is whether or not the business will continue to be profitable without you. If it isn't profitable, will your team lose their jobs? Will your fellow shareholders lose their income?

One Tuesday evening in May 2007, I was playing golf with my usual group. One of them, a keen dabbler in picking shares, collared me on the first tee.

"I've got a question about my money for you. Have you heard that Philip Carter has died?" he said.

"Philip who?" I replied.

"The MD of Carter and Carter. The training company that's based in Peterborough." As soon as someone talks to me about their money in this way, I know what question is coming next. "So, Charlie, do you think I should sell my shares in Carter and Carter?"

At the time, I knew nothing of this company, or the man who ran it, so I offered my generic advice in this instance: "That depends on how well he has set up the company, and how he has mitigated risks like his own death."

Philip Carter was a non-executive director of Chelsea FC. Like his chairman, Mathew Harding, he sadly died in a helicopter crash coming back from a Chelsea match, although this was not the same crash. He left behind his wife and children. His day job was running Carter and Carter, a highly successful training company that was valued at £500 million the day before his death.

The shares dropped in value by about 20% upon the news of his death, but within six months the shares had fallen from £12.75

to 85p and were suspended on the stock exchange. Less than 12 months later, in April 2008, the administrators were called in and the business folded.

His wife, instead of inheriting a business worth £500m, got nothing; the employees were out of a job; and had there been other shareholders in the business, they would have lost their stakes too.

This is just one example of the risks that business owners often overlook, but what could have been done?

One solution is known as Key Person Insurance. When something unexpected happens, like the death or serious illness of a shareholder or key member of the team, people get worried. The bank gets worried and may recall the overdraft. Creditors get worried and may pull their credit. Customers get worried and may be tempted to switch to one of the competitors, who you can guarantee will be swooping around like vultures. Employees get worried, as they have lost one of their key leaders. All this can put a company as successful as Carter and Carter out of business.

Key Person Insurance would have injected capital into the business to alleviate worries and provide liquidity in the short term, while replacements were recruited. This isn't just about the business owner either. What about your top salesperson? Will you lose business if they were to pass away or be incapacitated long-term? What about a key member of your leadership team? All this needs to be considered if you want your life's work to be able to live on beyond you.

Shareholder Protection

In addition to having protection in place to help support the business, having protection in place to support your family and other shareholders also makes sense. If you were to die, would your spouse want to be sat on the board of your company? How would your fellow shareholders feel about that? Would your spouse prefer the capital value of the shares and leave the company to be run by the remaining directors? All these questions need to be thought through and agreed. Once they have been, a Cross Option Agreement will probably be needed - a document that triggers the sale of the shares should either party want to sell. This combined with Shareholder Protection, to ensure there is sufficient money to purchase the shares at the pre-agreed price, would then also be sensible.

The Business Will

As a business owner, there are several reasons why a simple Will may not be sufficient, and a more comprehensive Business Will might be required. Reasons for this might include scenarios where the business must cease trading upon the owner's death, or where you might wish to appoint different people to administer your business to those for your personal estate, or for Inheritance Tax efficiency. I'll cover more about tax-saving strategies in the next section in line with the Trust Framework. These strategies are an important consideration, as they could save your future generations 40% on the value of your business.

The Contingency Plan

At Efficient Portfolio we have a document called 'The Contingency Plan', which documents what you would want to happen in your business following your demise. It is worth creating your own version of this document. The questions you need to ask yourself will depend on the size and structure of your business, but here are some starting points:

Who will run the business immediately after your death?

Who will run the business over the longer term?

Should the company be sold? If so, who do you think would be the best buyers?

How could you ensure your key relationships are maintained?

Is everything you do inside the business documented in an operations manual?

How would your bank / debtors / creditors react if the business changed hands?

How would your customers react?

Would there be enough money in the business to offset lost revenue or recalled debts?

Who *would* own the shares, and who *should* own the shares?

There is so much more to think about with a business, so it is worth spending some time ensuring that there is a plan in place in case the worst was to happen. It could be the difference between your business vanishing into a cloud of dust or going on to become your greatest legacy.

Section 2:

The Don't W.A.I.T. Protection Plan

W   Will

A   Attorney

I   Inherit

T   Trust

"Carve your name on hearts, not tombstones. A legacy is etched into the minds of others and the stories they share about you."

Shannon Adler, author

Chapter 6: Where There's a Will

I want to start off by diving into what we call 'The Don't W.A.I.T Protection Plan', because with estate planning it can certainly be too late if you do wait. When it comes to your finances, there are some planning opportunities that you can leave for the future, but estate planning is a pressing matter, because if something unexpected happens to you, your partner, or both, it could be too late. The opportunities are lost. The tax will be paid. The money will go to the wrong person, or the legal nightmare will begin. Whatever it is, it's too late, which is why it's vital that you 'don't wait'. You need to implement the ideas in The Don't W.A.I.T. Protection Plan as soon as they are appropriate to your life, and then they can lie dormant until the time when they are needed.

The first step is probably the most obvious: ensure you have written a Will. There are so many stories out there about the devastation and destruction caused to families when someone has died unexpectedly without a Will, or even where they have a 'DIY' Will, which I don't want to clog up these pages with! Instead, I will steal the words of a friend of mine who is a retired Financial Planner in Australia.

Peter Graham is retired from financial advice now, but he still coaches people on how to create a brilliant retirement. He understands death better than most because, in his 70's, he was given literally days to live as a result of incredibly aggressive cancer. He had a very slim chance of recovery through a specific type of treatment, but his greatest challenge was surviving the few days in between diagnosis and when the treatment could begin.

I was chatting to him once about people dying without a Will. To paraphrase, his words were 'anyone who dies without a Will should be turned away from the gates of Heaven until they have witnessed the pain and suffering they have inflicted upon their loved ones.' A typical Aussie not mincing his words, but it has stuck with me ever since!

Most sensible people have a Will. It makes sure that when you die, what you want to happen to your money actually does. If you don't create a Will, then you are deemed to have died 'Intestate' and your wealth, your property and any investments will follow a set process that may not deliver what you wanted, either now or in the future. Essentially, that means that you leave the Government to decide who gets your wealth. Not only that, but the people who you leave behind have an awful lot more pain and misery sorting out what happens. The following flow diagram will walk you through the Intestate Process:

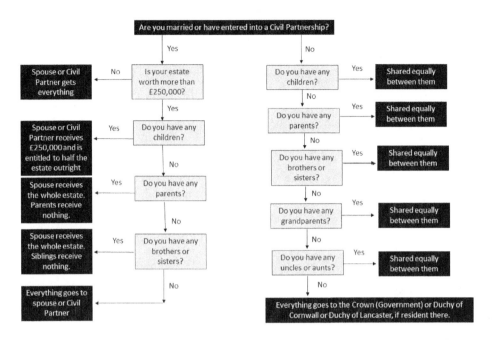

I often hear people say, "It'll all just go to my spouse if I don't have a Will". In reality, that often doesn't happen, as you can see from the diagram. What can end up happening is suddenly your children own a share of the family home, and there's actually been examples where widows have had to sue their own children to be able to get the property that they should have inherited. Had there just been a Will in place, it would have avoided this disastrous scenario for everyone. So, like I say, most sensible people do complete a Will, or ensure their Will is up-to-date. You can't go back and write a Will after someone has died, so therefore it's incredibly important to get your Will written, regardless of your age and circumstances.

A Will doesn't just have to be about the obvious stuff like who inherits your house but try and avoid being too clever. There was once an anonymous donation 'to clear the national debt': a public-spirited donor made a half-million-pound bequest to Britain back in 1928, which is now worth more than £350m. Unfortunately, the anonymous donor was very specific about how the money should be spent and stated that it should only be passed on once it was sufficient to clear the entire national debt. Sadly, the total national debt currently stands at £1.5tn and so the country can't touch the money.

The moral of the story is that being too specific can cause problems as time change. I once met a client whose father had changed his Will shortly before death to ensure that his wealth was not squandered. In an act that had nothing but the best intentions at its heart, he stated his wealth was to be placed in Trust and invested in Interest Bearing Bonds, with only the income generated being paid to his Beneficiaries. That was at a time where interest rates were around 8%, and Interest-Bearing Bonds were a reasonable and secure investment. Sadly, for the last 13 years interest rates have been close to zero, so the returns of such bonds have been incredibly low. Despite going to the highest court in the land, his Beneficiaries cannot undo this last instruction, cannot access any of the capital, and can only draw out the pittance that is the interest. Be careful of being too specific in your requests, as they may unintentionally backfire.

At Efficient Portfolio we work with a range of law firms to create a solution that works for you. If you'd like us introduce you, please don't hesitate to contact us at www.efficientportfolio.co.uk or hello@efficientportfolio.co.uk.

Chapter 7: Saved by Attorneys

The second step in The Don't W.A.I.T. Protection Plan is to make sure that if something unexpected happens to you, for example you're in an accident or you're taken seriously ill, then the people around you can make the right decisions on your behalf.

One day, a gentleman's wife was planning on hosting a dinner party and wanted to add a touch of class to the evening, so she sends her husband out to pick up some escargot. He dutifully heads out, picks up the snails and starts heading home, but on the way the gentleman runs into an old friend and stops to chat for a minute.

Rather than chew the fat in the street, the friend suggests, "Fancy a pint?" To which the gentleman replies, "No, I should really be getting back; my wife will kill me if I'm late for her dinner."

After some gentle prodding, the gentleman, of course, goes out for that one pint with his friend, snails in hand. The fellas get drinking and lose track of time, drinking through the afternoon and into the evening, until the gentleman looks up at the clock and exclaims, "Damn it! I'm 4 hours late for the dinner!" So, he snatches up his bag of snails and tears down the street towards home.

As the man approaches his house, stumbling and most definitely inebriated, he trips on the front step, resulting in a cacophonous crash, alerting his wife to his beleaguered predicament. She bangs open the door, looks down at the drunk, and explodes in a torrent of rage.

"Where the hell have you been?! You're 4 hours late for dinner! Explain yourself, you drunken sot!"

The gentleman, clothes disheveled, and snails strewn haphazardly on his front lawn, knows he's in serious trouble and decides to try his luck. Squatting down and clapping his hands, he booms, "Come on! Five feet more lads, we're almost there!"

This gentleman, even when he was in a sorry old state, was sufficiently capable of getting himself out of trouble. Whilst this tale is hopefully amusing and lighthearted, it does help to illustrate a very serious point: capability is what is required in our worst moments, so that we can maintain our wealth and our wellbeing. If we no longer have that capability, or lose our capacity to make decisions, we will need someone to make decisions on our behalf. It is for this reason that we all need a Lasting Power of Attorney (LPA).

An LPA is a legal document that allows you (the Donor) to appoint someone you trust (the Attorney) to make decisions on your behalf in circumstances where you lack the permanent or temporary capacity or overall capability to do so. There are 2 types of LPA: one for Property and Financial Affairs and the other for Health and Welfare.

With a Property and Financial Affairs LPA, your Attorneys can act for you in transactions such as buying and selling property, opening and closing bank accounts, dealing with your investments, managing your day-to-day finances, and claiming benefits and pensions. While you are still mentally capable, they can only implement your wishes and they must help you to make your own decisions, even if they don't necessarily agree with them. Only if you lose mental capacity and capability will they be able to make decisions on your behalf.

A Health and Welfare LPA enables your attorneys to make decisions about where you should live, your day-to-day care and to give consent to, or refuse, medical treatment on your behalf. This type of LPA is very important for unmarried couples who want to ensure that they are the ones who can make these decisions for their partners rather than their other half's family members stepping in.

If you are married, in a Civil Partnership or a relationship, you don't have to make both LPA's, but it does make sense to do both just in case. Ensuring an LPA is in place will mean that decisions can be made quickly by someone you trust if you ever lose mental capacity or capability, and your affairs can be looked after even if you find yourself physically or mentally unable to do so.

You may think that because you've got a joint bank account it would be all fine, and your spouse or partner would be able to just carry on using it. In reality, we're starting to see examples where if one of the account holders is incapacitated, the banks are freezing the account if there's not an LPA in place. The reason behind this is that the unaffected account holder would effectively be making decisions on the incapacitated person's behalf, without their legal consent.

Lasting Powers of Attorney are incredibly important if you want to make sure that, if something unexpected happens, the people who you trust can care for you. If you don't have an LPA, your loved ones will be left having to apply to the Court of Protection to appoint a deputy. It can be a long and expensive struggle to gain access to vital funds and the ongoing costs can drain your assets dry. If a serious crisis has occurred, family members could struggle to gain access to your much needed funds, which they can only do by way of court order. LPAs, which cost a fraction of the amount charged by the Court of Protection, can avoid all the stress, intrusion, and expense involved in appointing a deputy.

If you don't have an LPA you have no say in who the court appoints as your deputy, and you also have no say in the scope of power granted to your deputy. In some cases, the deputy's application could also be refused, so the council may be appointed instead. Also, your family will have to pay extra to apply for and maintain a deputyship, and you may not be able to sell jointly held assets until the court appoints a deputy. The solution is to set up an LPA and give the people you trust the opportunity to do the best by you in your time of need.

At Efficient Portfolio we work with a range of experienced solicitors, who can help draft appropriate LPAs on your behalf. If you'd like us introduce you, please don't hesitate to contact us at www.efficientportfolio.co.uk or hello@efficientportfolio.co.uk.

Chapter 8: Inherit to the Max

They say that the light at the end of the tunnel is the tax man holding a torch. Personally, it's not an image I relish, and I certainly don't like the idea of my family's intended legacy ending up in the clutches of the Chancellor! If, like me, you want your loved ones to receive as much of your legacy as possible, you first need to understand the basic principles around how Inheritance Tax (IHT) works.

But isn't this tax something that only the financial elite face? Sadly, no. In reality, IHT is being paid by more and more people, so you may well be caught by it even if you don't consider yourself to be 'wealthy'. If you want to avoid the Chancellor becoming your single largest benefactor, you need to understand how IHT works, and how you can best minimise it.

Of course, you might not want to minimise IHT. You might want to hand a large chunk of your wealth over to the state. We do find that some people are keen to pay their share and that is a good thing, but when we talk through how the system works, we often find that rather than hand it to the Government and allow them to spend it as they will, people would prefer to be more specific and select a charity or charities, so that the money is spent in areas that mean something to them. So, whilst that's something to consider, we find most people want to generate the maximum inheritance possible for their next generation, as they feel that they've already paid sufficient tax during their lifetime.

To be able to talk through Inheritance Tax planning, it's important that you understand the principles of IHT. IHT is currently set at 40% and is applicable on any estates that exceed an allowance that we all get, which is called the 'Nil Rate Band' (NRB). The Nil Rate Band currently sits at £325,000 per person, or £650,000 per married couple, and has stagnated at this level since 2009. For each of us, the first £325,000 (or £650,000) is exempt from IHT, but we pay 40% on anything above that.

Because the Nil Rate Band hasn't been increased in line with inflation (unlike the growth on investments, property prices and general incomes) more and more people are exposed to IHT. It's also likely that the NRB will remain at £325,000 for the foreseeable future.

Some good news though is that we also have what's called the Residential Nil Rate Band (RNRB), which is an add-on to the NRB that takes the allowance up to a total of £500,000 per person, which means that a couple receive £1m allowance. The bad news is that the RNRB is a bit more complicated than the NRB. It is linked to you owning property that you intend to leave to a child or a remoter lineal descendant (e.g., a grandchild, great grandchild etc.) It also tapers out when your estate is worth between £2.35m and £2.7m, therefore larger estates don't qualify for it at all.

Just to make things even more complicated, in addition to the NRB and the RNRB, we also have certain allowances that we can utilise to minimise IHT during our lifetimes. An individual can make a tax-exempt £3000 gift each year, and any unused allowance for the previous year can be rolled over if the full allowance wasn't utilised. This is known as your 'Annual Exemption'. So, if you didn't use any of last year's allowance, you could make a £6,000 gift this year without worrying about any IHT implications.

For further complexity, you can also make as many gifts of up to £250 as you like to different people, without IHT implications, and you can make normal gifts out of your income (for example as Christmas presents) as long as you maintain your normal standard of living after having made the gift. There are also certain situations, like the marriage of a child or grandchild, where you can make a gift without IHT implications; however, there are caps on how much you can gift (£5,000 for a child, £2,500 for a grandchild, and £1,000 for anyone else). In addition, if you give money to charity, then that will be free of Inheritance Tax.

Finally, there is also a very important rule called 'Spousal Exemption', which enables spouses and Civil Partners to pass across unlimited assets free of Inheritance Tax. Now there is something very important to point out here. If you're not married or in a Civil Partnership, and you wish to leave your assets to your partner, they will end up paying Inheritance Tax.

A friend of mine sadly lost her partner in her 40's. They weren't married. They had been together for many years and were living in a house together that he owned. He left the property to my friend in his Will but had not considered IHT. As such, she was required to pay IHT to remain living in their home of many years. If you're not married, be really careful around how you structure this, and seek advice, but if you are married assets passing between the two of you are free of IHT.

One easily missed planning opportunity is that there is also an exemption for regular gifts out of 'excess income'. You can make gifts out of income, as long as it's a regular gift, it comes out of income not capital, and it doesn't affect your standard of living. As long as you meet those criteria, it is a nice way to get money outside of your estate immediately without IHT implications; but remember to document this so that there's a consistent record following your death, which many people often overlook.

Something that people generally are more aware of, but often don't really understand, are the rules around gifting capital. Making a gift of capital is called a 'Potentially Exempt Transfer' or PET. A PET is where you make a gift of some capital, like money or property, to one of your children and as long as you live for 7 years, it will be free of IHT. That is why it is 'potentially exempt', as it is only completely free from IHT if you live for 7 years after having made the gift. If you die within those 7 years, people often think that the gift tapers down, which is partially true but not the full story. The tapering does exist, but it is only for gifts over the NRB, so currently gifts of more than £325,000. Gifts under this value will be fully taxable if you die within the 7 years. Again, it is sensible to document these gifts, so that they cannot be classed as a loan.

It is the prospect of PETs that led the former Chancellor, Roy Jenkins to say that "Inheritance Tax is a voluntary levy paid by those who distrust their heirs more than they dislike the Inland Revenue," because in theory you could give all of your money away. Of course, there are positives and negatives of using PETS. On the plus side, they are simple, easy, free to do and as long as you live for 7 years, very effective for saving IHT.

On the flip side of this argument, once you've made a gift, that's it, the control has gone; you've given it up. If the benefactor was to spend it frivolously or get married, then divorced, it's gone. Also, once the money has been gifted, will you have enough to live on? How much money will you need for your own future and lifetime? It's all about balance.

PETs are good in some ways, but that lack of control, the worry about not knowing when would be the right time to part with your money or lacking the knowledge of whether or not you will live for 7 years limit their use.

I mentioned that gifts to charities are free from IHT, but that isn't the only way you can use charitable donations to reduce the IHT payable on your death. If you are willing to give 10% of your entire estate to charity, you can reduce your IHT rate down from 40% to 36%. If you are going to make a gift to a charity in your Will anyway, then gifting 10% makes a lot of sense, as it means you can maximise your money's impact whilst minimising the effect on your Beneficiaries. We did some calculations for a client recently that showed that their Beneficiaries were only giving up 17 pence in the pound for them donating 10% of their estate to charity because of this saving, so it was a sensible strategy for their situation.

How Much Is Enough for Me?

One of the most difficult concepts around IHT planning is actually the question I posed earlier in this chapter: how much do you need for your lifetime? How can you contemplate giving money away if you don't know how much you will need? This is often what stops people making gifts early enough for them to be effective from a tax perspective.

When I first moved to London, two friends and I decided we were going to head down to Brighton for the weekend to go to a party. This was well before the likes of Sat Navs and Google Maps, so ordinarily we would have opted for more traditional navigation, but for whatever reason I didn't have a road map in my car. I had achieved a gold Duke of Edinburgh Award only a few years before, and I thought my sense of direction was pretty good, so with an air of confidence off we went. We set off from Chiswick, West London, and aimed South, which we thought would be about right, and hoped the road signs would do the rest.

Excited about the prospect of a party, my female passengers happily chatted in the back of the car, but sadly didn't offer me much assistance, so we managed to get off to a pretty bad start. We found the M3, and headed out of London thinking that would take us to the right route. The lack of signs for Brighton caused us some mild concern, but we concluded that Portsmouth must be just next door to our destination, so we would head there and pick up the right road. The problem was that the further we travelled along this route, the more damage we did to our overall journey. After driving for more than an hour, when the total journey should take about an hour and a half, we accepted defeat. Eventually we found a garage, stopped, bought a map, and asked where we actually were. A rather amused cashier pointed us to the correct page, and then the correct road.

By this point, we had gone so far off route that it took us nearly 2 hours to get to Brighton, and we had missed half of the party! The mistake we made was that we didn't plan the route beforehand, and we didn't have anything to ensure we kept on track. Nowadays, we would have looked at the route in advance, and then used a Sat Nav to keep us on track and make adjustments to any errors we made.

This sounds obvious doesn't it, but in actual fact most people spend their life managing their finances in the same way I approached my journey to the party in Brighton. Most people go through their life not really knowing what their financial future looks like. Isn't that like trying to drive to Brighton by only focusing on the next corner? They can see what they have now, and how their decisions have affected their money in the past by looking in the rear-view mirror, but they do not look further ahead than the next corner or signpost when it come to their finances. In order to get to Brighton, you need to plan the journey before you set off, so you have an idea of how you are going to get there. Ideally, you then need a Sat Nav to ensure you keep looking at the bigger picture to make sure you arrive safely.

When it comes to their finances, people get lost, and most don't get to where they wanted to go. In fact, where they end up isn't where they wanted to be at all. Because of the odd wrong turn along the way, they end up in Portsmouth instead of Brighton. Whilst they are not a million miles away from where they wanted to be, to undo those wrong turns isn't quick and easy. Whilst on a car journey this might not be the end of the world, with your money this could mean that you run out during your lifetime, or you could be dying the richest person in the graveyard, leaving your children with a huge IHT bill, and having not done some of the things you always dreamed of.

The question is, when it comes to your finances, what is your financial Sat Nav? Believe it or not, it does exist! It is known as a Lifetime Cash-Flow Forecast. A Lifetime Cash-Flow Forecast gives you the clarity of what your financial future could look like. It hypothesises how future events could fit into your life, allowing you to build in the aspects that are important to you, so that you can see how they will impact your financial future. It allows you to make more informed decisions because you can see the impact such events may have on your future.

Lifetime Cash-Flow Forecasting enables you to visualise your current wealth, and how life decisions may affect your wealth over time. It is vital in financial planning, as it helps you gain greater clarity around your financial future.

When we are building Lifetime Cash-Flow Forecasts for our clients, we assume everyone is going to live to age 100. It's unlikely they all will, but some very well could. If we assumed life ended at say 93, and then they are the one that lives to 100, they would have too much life at the end of their money, and that is best avoided!

A Lifetime Cash-Flow Forecast is an incredibly powerful tool when it comes to maximising your legacy and minimising the IHT your beneficiaries pay. It is the tool that, once you have mastered it, allows you to make gifts or use estate planning strategies during your lifetime, knowing that you will have enough for your needs, even if you need to spend your final years in an expensive care home. Benjamin Franklin said that "If you fail to plan, you are planning to fail!" And this certainly applies to your money, especially when you are trying to find the balance between having enough for yourself and being able to leave a legacy during your lifetime.

At Efficient Portfolio we have been building our clients Lifetime Cash-Flow Forecasts for many years and they form a key part of 'The S.A.F.E. Retirement Roadmap', a system that allows our clients to see into their financial future more clearly to allow them to make better decisions about tomorrow today. If you don't currently have a Lifetime Cash-Flow Forecast, you can see a video explanation and some examples at www.efficientportfolio.co.uk/what-is-lifetime-cashflow-forecasting

Eroded by Inflation

Have you noticed that things keep getting more and more expensive? When I was at school, a Double Decker, my favourite chocolate bar because of that delightful combination of wispy nougat, a crispy base and lashings of Cadbury's milk chocolate, cost me 18p. I distinctly remember this, because, unlike a Snickers, my second favourite sweet treat, it cost under 20p.

That meant I could even throw in a couple of cola bottle penny sweets. The things we remember!

Anyway, back to the point: a Double Decker used to cost 18p, but it now costs 60p; over 3 times the price. That would be acceptable if the product had improved, but no. Not only is it over 3 times the price, but it is also now smaller than it was in my formative years. The Double Decker has been eroded over time! This isn't limited to this particular product; we now get one less Jaffa Cake than we used to in a packet, and fewer Maltesers to boot. I assume we get fewer Revels too, but I dare say they still throw in those horrid coffee ones to make it like the Russian Roulette of confectionary!

This trend of erosion isn't confined to sweet treats, it happens to our money too. Not only that, but for the last 13 years that trend has been accelerating. You'll be keenly aware that the interest rate you are paid by the bank is close to zero, however inflation continues to average around 2%. If you are lucky enough to get 1% interest from your bank, but inflation is 2%, that means that your money is still falling by 1% each year in real terms, i.e. what you can buy with it. Whilst from one year to the next the savings account may still stay at roughly the same amount, your purchasing power has fallen. It is shrinking, like my beloved Double Decker.

If you want your loved ones to inherit the greatest legacy possible, you've got to make sure that your capital is growing at a rate faster than inflation, otherwise you are guaranteed to have your wealth eroded. Also, the longer it goes on for, the greater the impact.

Chris, my Best Man, lives in Singapore. When he was over a few years ago, we said we would go and swing the clubs in anger and play some golf. Having not seen each other for a while, there was the usual banter flying around. You know the sort of thing: I'd say, "You know your problem is that you stand too close to the ball…. after you've hit it". He'd come back with, "It's a dead sheep… still ewe!"

Anyway, Chris is an Investment Banker, so, as the reputation goes, is a little reckless with money. On the other hand, with my role, I need to be cautious with money. Walking up the first tee he said we ought to be playing this golf match for money. "Chris", I said, "I do not need any extra reason to play bad golf, so please, let's not."

"Charlie," he retorted, "you are a successful businessman, and I am sure you can cope with playing golf for a little money."

"Chris, if we must, OK, but let's just play for 10p per hole."

"10p a hole sounds a little pathetic," he says, "let's do that but double it each hole".

"Ok", I reluctantly agreed.

On the first hole, which I think I lost, we were playing for 10p, but hey, as he said, I'm a successful businessman, so I could cope with that. On the second hole we are playing for 20p, so not too much stress there either. 40p on the 3rd and 80p on the fourth were also fine with me. By the 7th though, I am starting to shake over the putts, as we are now playing for £6.40 a hole, but I am playing reasonable golf, so I am confident I can take it off him. However, it quickly starts getting out of hand from here on in.

By the 10th we were playing for £51 per hole, and that was too much for me, so I called the betting a day, but it certainly made me think about what was going to happen if we continued. By the 16th we would have been playing for £3,276, and on the 18th we would have been playing for £13,107 just for that hole! Way too much for either of us to be entertaining. What started as

70

10p quickly escalated, which we certainly hadn't anticipated when we were walking down the first hole being all macho about playing for money.

So, what happened there? Well, this is what is known as compound growth. It is the effect of the growth on the growth on the growth. To look at it another way, if you look a standard piece of paper (0.05mm thick) and folded it in half 50 times, do you know how high it would reach? The answer is about 100 million kilometres, which is about two thirds of the distance between the Sun and the Earth. Amazing isn't it! That is compound growth at work.

If you can get you money benefiting from compound growth, you will reach financial freedom more quickly, and stay there for longer, so you need to find ways to get a bit more growth out of your money at every opportunity. An extra ½ % here or there may not sound that much, but over time it makes a massive difference.

This compound effect can also work against you though. When it comes to inflation, the erosion over time also compounds. If you are getting 1% less than inflation on the cash in your bank account, after 20 years over 18% of your capital will have been eroded away, which is why it is so important to get growth over and above inflation.

At Efficient Portfolio, we use a system called 'The R.A.D.I.C.A.L. Investment Approach' to help our clients get the best growth possible for a level of risk they are comfortable with. You may say you aren't comfortable with any risk, but as you've just seen, leaving your money in the bank will expose it to erosion, which is a risk all by itself. There really isn't such a thing as 'no risk'.

As a business, we aim to ensure our clients benefit from the best returns possible within a properly diversified portfolio.

Warren Buffett, the most successful investor of all time, once said that the asset allocation, or the diversification of your investments, is the most important investment principle of all. And we agree.

If you want to find out more about The R.A.D.I.C.A.L. Investment Approach, I talk through the principles in an online course called 'The Life Legacy Roadmap', which you can subscribe to for free at www.efficientportfolio.co.uk/life-legacy-roadmap-course

At Efficient Portfolio we also created 'The 2 Minute Retirement Plan', which is an online tool that produces a very basic Lifetime Cash-Flow Forecast. You can access it for free at www.efficientportfolio.co.uk/tools/the-2-minute-retirement-plan

Chapter 9: In Family You Trust

Now that you understand a little more about IHT, it would be prudent to look at some of the ways you can proactively ensure your Beneficiaries pay less of it, as that way you can create a bigger legacy without spending less or saving more.

An important caveat though before we proceed: 'tax avoidance' and 'tax planning' are all above board and are endorsed by the Government; whereas 'tax evasion' is illegal. I also believe that the days of using aggressive tax planning strategies, the likes of which had Jimmy Carr and Gary Barlow plastered all over the front pages, are gone. The Revenue have put in place 'Anti-Avoidance Legislation', so I urge you to steer clear of anything too aggressive, as it could land you in hot water.

All of the ideas in this chapter are very much mainstream planning opportunities and have a common theme of utilising the allowances you've been given. The strategies I will discuss are also all underpinned by the notion of ensuring that your assets pass down through your bloodline, rather than being lost to other parties. You'll be pleased to know that this chapter focusses on a lot more than just tax!

The Trust Framework

One of the most powerful tools that we can use to boost the amount of money that people inherit, and also to protect your wealth, is a Trust, using what we call a 'Trust Framework'. A Trust Framework can protect assets from all sorts of different threats, including the tax man, and can help to make sure your legacy goes to who you want it to, when you want it to, in a tax effective and protected way.

I mentioned in Chapter 6 that having a Will was really important, but a Will on its own is just not sufficient for most people. A Will allows your Executors to know exactly what you want to happen on the day you die; the problem is that's where it ends. A Will doesn't dictate what happens after the day you die, and that's where the problems arise.

To explain the problem of having just a Will, I want to use my own family situation. I'm married to Caryl, and we have two beautiful daughters, Ffion and Bronwyn, who are 14 and 12 at the time of writing. If I were to die, I would leave everything to Cary, and then when she passed away, she would want to leave it all to Ffion and Bronwyn, which all makes sense doesn't it? A Will would allow this to happen, but the problem is that often that isn't what ends up happening, but why is that?

Let's start off with the fact that after I die, there is a good chance that Caryl might remarry. Let's call him Juan, shall we? So, let's say Caryl remarries Juan, and then gets divorced. Well, that means Juan's walking off with 50% of Ffion and Bronwyn's inheritance. Or worse, maybe Caryl marries Juan and then she dies, and he walks off with all of their inheritance. Even if Caryl didn't remarry, but were to end up in a care home, then obviously all that that money will be spent on care fees. Then, as and when Caryl passes away, all of the assets left in her estate are liable for IHT purposes, which means it is likely that a fair chunk of Ffion and Bronwyn's inheritance goes to the tax man. The intention of my Will has not come to fruition in any of these scenarios.

You may think that's where the problems end, but it isn't. As I mentioned, at the moment Ffion and Bronwyn are just 14 and

12. If Caryl and I just had a Will and both of us passed away now, the money would be held for the girls, but on the day they turned 18 they would be entitled to the whole amount. Now that will probably lead to an amazing fresher's week, but not a very motivated life thereafter. I'm not saying my girls are reckless, but there might be a couple of Paris Hiltons running around, squandering their inheritance on parties, fast cars, and designer handbags! This is obviously a concern too. Caryl and I don't want our daughters inheriting too much too early, because it could well ruin their lives.

Even when the girls are a bit older and more responsible, by inheriting all of that money, they might attract the wrong sort of partner, and as a protective dad I'm obviously worried about that! If they married the son-in-law from hell and then get divorced, half of their money would disappear out of the family again. And then of course, as and when they want to leave it to their children, they've got IHT to worry about all over again.

So, a Will just isn't enough. It does what is needed the day that you die, but it doesn't protect the assets for the future generations after that. It doesn't ensure that those assets flow down the bloodline, and it doesn't ensure that they do so in a tax efficient way. This where we can use Trusts to help.

Trusts are often thought of as the preserve of the super-rich, but that is really not the case. Certainly, anybody in the territory of breaching the IHT allowance should be thinking about a Trust Framework. Actually, many people below that threshold should be considering Trusts too, purely for the bloodline protection benefits they provide. So how would a Trust Framework help in my family situation?

Firstly, upon my death, certain assets would pass immediately to the Trust Framework. That would be things like my life insurance, my pension, my shares in my business and also the first chunk of my estate, usually an amount equal to the Nil Rate Band, so currently £325,000.

All of those assets that go into the Trust Framework are made immediately available to Caryl, by way of an interest free loan. She can still spend or utilise those assets, so for example she could downsize the house or sell the business shares, if she wishes. It doesn't stop her spending the money, unless I want it to, but does ensure we ring fence certain assets so that if Caryl does remarry Juan, and then divorces or dies, we've managed to protect the assets for Ffion and Bronwyn. Equally, some protection from care fees has been achieved, and then as and when Caryl passes away, we've managed to protect certain assets against IHT. It hasn't fixed the entire problem, but we've managed to keep some assets outside of the estate and increase our legacy.

When it comes down to Ffion and Bronwyn, if they are still young in this situation, Caryl and I can put Trustees in place, who will have far better control over the assets and can ensure they are passed down at an appropriate time. For example, perhaps the Trustees decide that Ffion and Bronwyn shouldn't be able to access all of this capital at once, so an income is more suitable until they have finished their education. They help ensure that Ffion and Bronwyn can build a properly motivated life for themselves, which to me and Caryl is really important.

Even when the girls are old enough, they can become the Trustees themselves and make decisions about the capital, but they'd probably still be best to take the money out of the Trust as an interest free loan. That way, if they marry the son-in-law from hell and then divorce, those assets will be exempt from a divorce settlement, or at least there's the best chance possible of this happening. Finally, when they want to leave that money down to their children, they can return that money to the Trust and skip IHT on that particular money.

Using a Trust Framework really is an incredibly powerful planning tool. It allows you to protect some of your assets from the taxman, a future spouse and care fees, but also allows that money to move down through the bloodline, down through the generations, and stay within the family.

Have Your Cake

A Trust Framework is the first weapon in our arsenal for mitigating Inheritance Tax and protecting our financial legacy for the next generation, but there are some further steps we can take if we want to further reduce IHT. Whilst the Trust Framework mitigates some Inheritance Tax, it does not usually mitigate it all. There are other strategies out there that we can use to try to do that.

I often describe IHT planning as being like cake, and this is the case for two reasons: the first is that you can't have your cake and eat it; just like you can't give away a painting and then still leave it hanging on your wall, because you breach a rule called 'Gift with Reservation'.

To use the painting analogy, if said piece is adorning your wall, you can still see it and enjoy the beauty of it every day, even if you don't 'own' it. If this is the case, it's still technically yours (i.e., you're benefitting from it), and you haven't truly given it away, unless you pay the owner to rent it. It is the same with the property. You can't give a property away and then live in it unless you pay a commercial rent for the whole time that you live there. If you don't pay the rent, the house (the gift) will breach the rule, and from an IHT point of view will be ineffective.

In short, you can't give anything away and still benefit from it. With IHT planning, pretty much every strategy that I'm about to go through has some advantages and some disadvantages;

effectively you're giving up certain rights but you're also retaining certain rights.

I mentioned that Inheritance Tax Planning is like cake for two reasons. The second reason is because, very much like a cake, IHT planning is usually best done if you take a layered approach. For me, the best cakes have multiple layers, each containing different textures or flavours, therefore they satisfy our sweet tooth at a higher level.

A single type of IHT planning is unlikely to be the right solution for anyone, so no one of the ideas that I will briefly discuss are likely to solve all of your problems. The best approach is usually a blended, multi-faceted strategy.

Let's look at some of these ideas as to how you can mitigate IHT to boost your family's legacy.

The first option is a really straightforward approach. For this we need to revisit the Potentially Exempt Transfer (PET), the gift that takes 7 years to leave your estate but is tax free if you do. This time though, instead of giving this gift directly to the Beneficiary and giving up all control, you give it to a Trust. We call this the 'Protective Gifting Trust'. Because it is still technically a PET, it still needs 7 years to leave your estate, but the difference is that you retain control. You can be a Trustee, so you can make sure you can control when the gift becomes available. You can also protect the gift down through the bloodline, for example, shielding it from the clutches of the son or daughter-in-law from hell. It is quite a useful strategy, but it is fairly limited in it its use, as you are giving up capital or income for the rest of your life.

The next layer to your cake is a slight variation on the principle of gifting money into a Protective Gifting Trust and is called a 'Gift and Loan Trust'. A Gift and Loan Trust allows you to make a gift but retain access to the original capital. Let's say you've got

£100,000 that you want to keep, but you're happy to give away the growth on that money. By putting that £100,000 in the Gift and Loan Trust, all future growth on that money will be outside of your estate for IHT, but you can access the £100,000 as quickly or as slowly as you wish. Again, this strategy is only useful in certain situations, but it's another weapon in the artillery, or another layer to your cake.

The next layer you might want to consider is a bit of a step up and it's what's called a 'Discounted Gift Trust'. This is useful when you have capital you don't need for the rest of your life, but you do need to take an income from. The Discounted Gift Trust allows you to put the capital into the Trust, thereby saving some IHT immediately, because some of the money now falls outside of your estate.

The rest of the money falls outside of your estate over 7 years, as with a PET. The real perk here is that you can also draw an income, which is usually 5% of the capital that you put in. You retain that income during your lifetime, but if you die after 7 years, all of the remaining capital will be outside of your estate for IHT purposes.

The downside of a Discounted Gift Trust is that you must take the income; however, there is another slightly more complicated Trust based solution where the income becomes optional. This is called a 'Flexible Reversionary Trust'. This again can be a really useful layer to your legacy cake recipe.

Ultimately, the type of Trust or Trusts that you could utilise will depend on your individual situation, so it's strongly recommended to speak to a professional to assess what you may need.

What a Relief

All of those Trusts had some sort of restriction on them. You were either giving up access entirely or giving up access to some or all of the capital, so, like I said, you can't have your cake and eat it! The advantage of them is that once the capital is inside the Trusts, the money can be managed and invested as you would have chosen to do so outside of that framework. For example, you could employ all the principles of The R.A.D.I.C.A.L. Investment Approach.

Another way you can save IHT is to use what's called 'Business Property Relief' (BPR), which won't be suitable for everyone. Business Property Relief is a strategy that's put in place to allow business owners to pass on their business intact to the next generation, or shareholders of qualifying companies to reduce their IHT bill. A similar relief for farmers exists called 'Agricultural Property Relief'.

BPR applies to shares on unlisted businesses and companies listed on the Alternative Investment Market (AIM); so not FTSE 100 or FTSE 250 companies, but smaller businesses. The AIM market is an example of such smaller businesses, which contains companies like Naked Wines, Fever Tree Tonic, or internet clothing retailer ASOS. The benefit of holding shares like these, or even agricultural land or your own business property, is that they qualify for Business Property Relief once you've owned them for 2 years, at which point they become zero rated for IHT purposes. The benefit here is that you can still own the investment, so you can still sell it, spend the capital, or access the income, if required.

But of course, you can't have your cake and eat it here either! The downside is that these types of investments tend to be risky and are not suitable for most people concerned with IHT planning. I find that most people who come to me with a priority of IHT planning don't want to be taking risks with their money, so therefore an AIM listed portfolio of investments like this is not usually appropriate. Sadly, these types of investments are pushed onto unwitting retirees all too often for my liking. It's great to reduce the IHT on your estate by 40%, but if the investments fall by 50%, and these could, it somewhat defeats the objective!

However, there a good way of gaining access to Business Property Relief without taking quite as much risk as an AIM portfolio, setting up your own business or buying agricultural land. There are Business Property Relief Investments out there that try to minimise risk as much as possible. They are still risky, so you wouldn't want this to be the only layer in your cake, but it brings another flavour to the planning for some people. The risk is a different type of risk to a traditional portfolio, so it's not right for everybody, but the investments do tend to be slightly more secure. For example, there may be an investment opportunity for a company backing solar panel projects, where the returns are provided by the Government's Feed in Tariff. Again, these types of investments certainly aren't right for everybody, but they are a way of qualifying for Business Property Relief whilst trying to keep the risk manageable.

All of the strategies I've talked about so far are generally not aggressive; they're very much mainstream planning that the Revenue endorse, because ultimately all you're doing is using up your allowances or helping smaller companies.

Last Chance Saloon

For people who have multiple properties, or a large family home, I appreciate that I probably haven't been much help so far, because properties and Trusts don't really mix that well. For example, if you gift property into Trust, you could end up paying a load of tax during your lifetime; plus, the Trust will force you to pay a higher rate of taxation than you might've done personally.

If you own multiple properties, or indeed one high-value home, it can be quite difficult to plan your way out of IHT. For owners of multiple properties, we quite often find that people, especially in retirement, end up selling their buy-to-let properties because of the principles with The R.A.D.I.C.A.L. Investment Approach, and also so they can plan for IHT much more effectively. But if selling isn't an option, especially if it's your family home, there is one 'last chance saloon' to mitigate IHT, and that is to insure the tax liability.

Let's imagine you own a few homes, and we work out that the Inheritance Tax liability would equate to £500,000. When you die, your children or Beneficiaries would have to sell that property, or properties, so that they could pay the tax liability before they could inherit your estate. This is of course a viable option, but selling an illiquid asset, such as bricks and mortar, can take a lot of time, and can of course cost money to do so. This process also means that your Beneficiaries can't touch their inheritance for an indeterminable period of time.

There is an alternative though. What you could do is put in place a policy where you pay a monthly premium. In this example, on the day you die, the policy pays out £500,000 and this goes into a Trust, waiting to pay the tax; whether it be next year or whether it be in 30 years' time. It's essentially a type of insurance, but it's a great way of mitigating IHT whilst not disturbing your assets.

A lot of our industry will use this as the first port of call for IHT planning. My instinct is that you are actually better to try and mitigate as much tax as possible with the tools I've described earlier on, and then insure the residual liability.

However, this type of solution does provide us with an opportunity to create an even better legacy for your next generation. For a relatively small amount of money each month, you have the opportunity to create a lump of money in a Trust for the people who you care most about. So, sometimes clients will use this strategy, particularly if they've got an income that exceeds what they spend each month, to turn that income into a legacy for the next generation.

The key to The Don't W.A.I.T. Protection Plan is that you mustn't wait! All of these opportunities to protect your wealth and create an amazing legacy are lost if something serious or fatal happens. It's vital that you get the right layers of the cake in place as soon as possible, to ensure that what you want to happen does, and in the most tax efficient and protected way.

At Efficient Portfolio we created' The 1 Minute Wealth Protector'- an online tool that can help you identify how you can better protect your wealth. You can access it for free at www.efficientportfolio.co.uk/tools/the-1-minute-wealth-protector

Don't wait, and you can create an incredible legacy that can help generations to come.

Section 3:

The L.A.S.T. Gift

L   Legend

A   Advice

S   Spirit

T   Today

"The things you do for yourself are gone when you are gone, but the things you do for others remain as your legacy."

Kalu Ndukwe Kalu, political scientist

Chapter 10: Passing on the Legend

If you look up the word 'Legend' in the dictionary, the following definitions come up:

- a nonhistorical or unverifiable story handed down by tradition from earlier times and popularly accepted as historical;
- the body of stories of this kind, especially as they relate to a particular people, group, or clan;
- an inscription, especially on a coat of arms, on a monument, under a picture, or the like;
- a table on a map, chart, or the like, listing and explaining the symbols used;
- a collection of stories about an admirable person.

All of these beautifully sum up what I mean by 'The Legend' that I refer to in this chapter. At times you may not believe it, but we all lead such interesting lives, particularly to those who live in a different context, culture, or environment. For example, when we hear stories about our grandparents' childhoods, the everyday occurrences that they may have found relatively commonplace or mundane, are fascinating and enthralling for us to hear.

When she was in her 90's, my grandma wrote up a few pages to give her family an insight into what life was like for her growing up. I was living in London at the time and remember reading the version that was typed up by a friend of hers. Grandma's 'memoir' started off by her talking about what life was like at school: walking 2 ½ miles each way, every day, which is something that seems quite alien nowadays. She then went on to tell the tale of her adult life, when her farm in Deene, Northamptonshire, became the residence of numerous army regiments during the Second World War, with tanks driving up and down their drive, and on one occasion, her shock when a bus load of Indian soldiers arrived. It is brilliant to be able to imagine what her farm looked like teaming with troops and gives the war I learnt about in textbooks and film a whole different perspective.

Whilst Grandma's write-up was relatively short, it was wonderful to take a small peek into a life that seems so far removed from today's world. When I came to write this book, Grandma's account instantly came to mind, followed by a sudden panic: did I have the only copy of that document, and if I did where was it now? Thankfully, I'd returned it to my mum for safe keeping, and better still was able revisit those wonderful stories nearly 20 years later.

My maternal grandfather, known as 'Gramp', on the other hand, was in the army during the Second World War. He didn't write up what happened to him during that time and, like a lot of young men of his generation, never really talked about it either. On asking Mum about Gramp's war experiences, or about his childhood, almost all the memories are gone. We don't even know whether he went to France or stayed stationed in the Orkney Islands. If he'd written up his 'legend', we would all know a lot more about his life.

There are two lessons to learn here. Firstly, for future generations it is really important to document in some way the key moments of your life. If you don't, they will be lost forever, like the stories I have no doubt Gramp had to tell. Secondly, once documented, it is vital they are stored somewhere permanent, so that they aren't lost by careless youths, accidents, or anything else. As humans we have a fascination with what came before us and learning about our wider and more personal history is an enriching experience. **The Life Legacy Planner** is a great place to start to build your legend and tell your story. Some questions that might help prompt you are in the Grandparent Interview section that follows.

The Grandparent Interviews

In my book 'The Dream Retirement', I talk about creating 'The Grandparent Interviews'. Wouldn't it be fantastic to have a video of your great-grandfather telling you about his life, what he learnt, and where the family has come from? What a wonderful thing to be able to share with future generations. Of course, we now have the opportunity to do all of that and create our own videos and audio recordings with nothing more than your mobile phone and a couple of apps.

If your parents are still alive, why not organise an interview with them to capture their magic moments? I am willing to bet you'll hear a few stories that you've never heard before! If your parents are no longer with us, record your own stories.

As part of **The Life Legacy Planner**, you can include the links to your Grandparent or Personal Interviews. Once recorded, you can upload them to www.Youtube.com , www.Vimeo.com or www.Wistia.com and save them as private if you wish. That way only people with the link will find them.

I passionately believe that this is something that each generation should do. Here are some questions that you might want to ask in your interview, or answer if you are doing it yourself:

1. Where did you grow up? What was it like growing up in your home and what funny stories can you remember of that time?
2. What were your hobbies and who did you do them with?
3. What great memories do you have of your school days? Who were your best friends?
4. What principles did your parents bring you up with?
5. What is the worst trouble you got into and why?
6. Tell me about each of your parents. What did they do, and how did they meet? What about their siblings too?
7. Tell me about each of your grandparents. Where did they live, what did they do? What about their siblings too?
8. What special memories do you have around people's birthdays, Christenings, weddings or Christmas?
9. What are your greatest memories as a family unit? What were your favourite and least favourite meals?
10. What family traditions did you have? Where did you spend family holidays, and what happened?
11. What did you do in the years immediately after leaving school?
12. How did you meet your wife/husband? What was your first impression, and what was dating like?
13. Where and when did you marry? Who were your bridesmaids and Best Man, and were there any funny stories from the day?
14. What were your early years of marriage like?
15. What was it like being a parent for the first time and what specific memories can you recall from these days?
16. Do you remember any other interesting stories from older generations?
17. What's the story you tell that gets the most laughs / evokes the most emotion?
18. If you could leave no money to your children, just a set of life principles, what would they be?

19. If you could live your life again, what if anything would you have done differently?
20. What is the funniest experience you've had in your life?
21. What advice would you give to your future generations?
22. What did you learn during your life that you wish you'd grasped earlier?

Ideally, get on and record your Grandparent Interviews, and be sure to save the links. You never know when it will be too late. That said, you can also use these questions to prompt your thoughts if you decide to write a book, create a scrapbook, record an audio account, or anything else for that matter.

As a couple of examples, you can see the interviews of my parents and parents in law here: www.efficientportfolio.co.uk/life-legacy-gift

If you want to read more about this, you can download a free copy of my book The Dream Retirement from **www.dream-retirement.com**.

Your Book

This is my fourth book, so it is easy to become complacent as to how surprisingly straightforward it can to write one, but I'm going to let you into a little secret. It took me just 4 weeks to write this book and we have published the book ourselves through Amazon, who will now print the number of copies we want to order. No lorry loads of copies to store somewhere, and we can print more whenever we want.

There has never been easier or cheaper to write a book. To prove a point, my nephew and godson, Toby, has published his very own readymade quiz book, at the age of 9! If there ever was a more exciting way to pass on your legend, a book has to be close to the top of the list. What better way to immortalise the story of your life? So here are my quick tips on how to best produce your very own 'Life Book':

1. Write a list of the funniest stories or anecdotes that have happened in your life. The ones you tell people down the pub. For inspiration here, see the next section.
2. Write a list of the most interesting things that have happened in your life. The ones you'd want to tell your grandchildren.
3. Write a list of the most emotional stories that have happened in your life. The ones that you wouldn't want to be forgotten and have possibly shaped the person you are today.
4. Write a list of the unusual things that have happened in your life. The ones that future generations might find hard to believe.
5. Write down a list of points you want to make, for example the values you have and any advice or wisdom you'd impart. Try to link each to one of the stories above. More on this in the next chapter.
6. Create a mind-map of the book. Use free software like www.miro.com to map out the above lists into a format, linking stories to points.
7. Put some time aside each week. It could be a day a week, a morning or even an hour.
8. Start writing. Procrastination is a fear of starting!
9. Think progress not perfection. People aren't going to worry if your grammar isn't perfect. They are more interested in what you have done and what you have to say.
10. If you find it easier, dictate or video the content. You can easily transcribe it to text using a service such as www.Rev.com, which is very cost-effective.

11. Good is good enough. Perfectionism is a fear of finishing, so don't strive for the perfect product. You can always revise it again in the future. Just get it out there.

12. In order to publish it really easily, I like to use Amazon Kindle Publishing, which allows you to produce a digital and physical version of your book. This platform provides step-by-step guidance on how to put your book together and gives you the option to design your own cover and artwork, if you don't want to have to pay for the services of a graphic designer. You can find out more here: www.kdp.amazon.com

    As a tip though, I'd recommend producing your document in a Word format in the size of book that you would like, for example A5. This document can then be simply uploaded and won't require lots of tweaks or adjustments.

Photographic Memories

During our life we all take lots of photos, but most of us don't have the time to organise or present them sufficiently well. Retirement is your chance to create a photo collection you and your future generations can be proud of. Never has there been such an opportunity to pass on so many memories of our life to our future generations with such ease. If you leave your children with photos all over the place, either printed or on your computer, they are more likely to be forgotten, damaged or lost. It can be difficult and time-consuming to organise your own photos, so just imagine organising someone else's! You have an opportunity to leave a legacy of your life with your photos, so seize it. To help ensure you leave your children a photographic legacy, not just an administrative headache, here are a few tips for you.

Get Your Photos Digitalised

If you have boxes and boxes of old photos, sort them! And then either scan them yourself or ask someone to do this for you. There are many photo-scanning websites out there, but one I have successfully used in the past is www.filmscanuk.co.uk. They will scan photos, slides and film, and return them to you on a CD.

Organise Them

If someone can't find your photos quickly, they'll stop looking. You need to organise them into a simple structure of folders and sub-folders so that when they want to look at something like your trip to New Zealand or a family wedding, they can, and quickly. The system that works best is to initially have a folder such as 'Holidays', 'Birthdays', 'Christenings and Weddings', 'Days Out' and so on. Within each folder there should be a sub-folder for each event or occasion by name and date, for example 'Venice 2015'. If you are looking to create an album (digital or printed), when you are sorting your photos create another sub folder called, unsurprisingly, 'Album' and add anything that you think should make the cut. Whether you actually make the album or not, you now quickly have access to the best photos you took without sifting through them all.

Personally, I am not one for deleting the non-album photos. You probably could, but for me, you just never know when you might want them. In this day and age, storage is so cheap and simple, I don't see a need to delete them, but if you wanted to make life simpler, you could.

Share and Enjoy Them

Now that you have the best photos organised into a selection of albums, enjoying them and sharing them becomes much easier. For example, if you want to put all of your best photos onto a digital picture frame, you could search 'My Pictures' for the word 'Album'. You then have all of your best photos in one, simple list that you can copy across to the SD card that goes into the picture frame. If you want to put them onto your tablet or any other device, you can follow a similar approach. If you want to show them to your family and friends, you can then use your tablet or computer and connect to the TV (the modern-day slide show, I suppose!)

The next way to enjoy them is to create an album. If you've ordered the prints online or from the local chemist, then that's fine, but you might want to take the considerable work out of building a physical photo album. There are loads of sites that will allow you to build photo books like www.bobbooks.co.uk and www.snapfish.co.uk. My favorite is www.myphotographics.co.uk. You download the software direct to your computer, so that you can build the book at your own speed, and you have a choice on the level of quality you need. Once you get the hang of the software, you can build these in no time at all with some quite spectacular results.

A photobook does not just have to be about your holiday or a particular event. You could also use the same concept to make a scrapbook of your life or your legend. That way you could include photos of people, places you visited, newspaper clippings and even stories you want to tell. Once done, you can print and reprint as many copies as you like, so they are never lost.

Back Them Up

You now have all of your photos on your computer in a beautifully organised folder system, which your family can look back on in decades or even centuries to come. Your life will never be forgotten—that is, until the computer dies, of course. But you can avoid this calamity by backing everything up. There's nothing worse than getting all of your photos into a beautifully organised system, only to lose them! Backing them up couldn't be simpler. You simply need to make sure that you have them in two places at any one time.

Depending on the size of your photo collection, these two locations could be your computer and online in the 'cloud'. Services such as 'Dropbox' www.dropbox.com, 'iCloud' www.icloud.com and 'Google Drive' www.google.com/drive allow you to synchronise your entire photo collection, and other documents for that matter, to the cloud. This means that you can access them anywhere, and if your computer dies, you don't lose anything.

In the long run, your family will thank you for managing your precious snaps this way, and your photographic legend will live on that much better as a result.

Chapter 11: Family Advice

Bronnie Ware, an Australian nurse who spent several years working in palliative care, caring for patients in the last 12 weeks of their lives, took the time to record their dying epiphanies into a book called 'The Top Five Regrets of the Dying.'

Ware writes of the amazing clarity of vision that people gain at the end of their lives, and how we might learn from their wisdom. "When questioned about any regrets they had or anything they would do differently," she says, "common themes surfaced again and again."

Here are the top five regrets of the dying, as witnessed by Bronnie Ware:

1. I wish I'd had the courage to live a life true to myself, not the life others expected of me.

"This was the most common regret of all. When people realise that their life is almost over and look back clearly on it, it is easy to see how many dreams have gone unfulfilled. Most people had not honoured even a half of their dreams and had to die knowing that it was due to choices they had made, or not made. Health brings a freedom very few realise, until they no longer have it."

2. I wish I hadn't worked so hard.

"This came from every male patient that I nursed. They missed their children's youth and their partner's companionship. Women also spoke of this regret, but as most were from an older generation, many of the female patients had not been breadwinners. All of the men I nursed deeply regretted spending so much of their lives on the treadmill of a work existence."

3. I wish I'd had the courage to express my feelings.

"Many people suppressed their feelings in order to keep peace with others. As a result, they settled for a mediocre existence and never became who they were truly capable of becoming. Many developed illnesses relating to the bitterness and resentment they carried as a result."

4. I wish I had stayed in touch with my friends.

"Often, they would not truly realise the full benefits of old friends until their dying weeks, and it was not always possible to track them down. Many had become so caught up in their own lives that they had let golden friendships slip by over the years. There were many deep regrets about not giving friendships the time and effort that they deserved. Everyone misses their friends when they are dying."

5. I wish that I had let myself be happier.

"This is a surprisingly common one. Many did not realise until the end that happiness is a choice. They had stayed stuck in old patterns and habits. The so-called 'comfort' of familiarity overflowed into their emotions, as well as their physical lives. Fear of change had them pretending to others, and to their selves, that they were content, when deep within, they longed to laugh properly and have silliness in their life again."

If these are the most common regrets before someone passes away, wouldn't it be better to pass these life lessons onto the people you care most about, so they don't make the same mistakes? I am sure over your life you have learnt some interesting lessons. If you share these lessons, your future generations can benefit from your experience and bypass all the learning journey you needed to go through to get where you ended up.

This is actually one of the main reasons that the Homo Sapiens evolved. Neanderthals were bigger, stronger and had bigger brains than Homo Sapiens, and so really had the odds stacked in their favour. Homo Sapiens, however, were more social than Neanderthals. That sociability allowed people to learn from others' experiences, thus accelerate what they could then achieve. The power and wisdom of the group massively advanced the species progress. Don't let your life's lessons be forgotten.

Now, advice is a funny thing. I don't know if you have children or not, but if you do and you've tried to give your children advice, it can be met with a mixed range of reactions. Occasionally it is the perfect advice at the perfect time, and it changes their approach forever. If only it was like that all of the time! With one teenager and one wannabe teenager in the house, more often than not my advice is not so warmly received!

For advice to strike a chord, it has to land at the right time. That is why writing it down or recording it in a video is so valuable, so that it is there whenever the time is right. Hopefully, that is during your lifetime, but sometimes that will be after you've gone. Take that document that my grandma put together about life in Deene during the war; when she wrote it, I was around 23 years old and partying in London was more of a priority than learning about the history of my family or our farm. Yet years later, I was keen to find out more, and to learn from her experience. Perhaps a more poignant example is the advice and lessons I learnt from my dad, David.

When I was a teenager, I was a fairly lazy child who was into heavy metal. If you've met me, I doubt you'd envisage me headbanging or playing the air guitar in my youth, but my bedroom walls were covered in Metallica, Iron Maiden and Guns 'n Roses posters for a good many years. When I was 16, my favourite band, Metallica, released a limited-edition box set that I decided I must have. It contained previously unreleased material of them playing live, and some other stuff that seemed incredibly important at the time. It of course came with an overinflated price tag, but the lure of how rare and exclusive this box set was only added extra weight to my desire to own it.

I asked my dad if he would buy it for me, and unsurprisingly was met with a less than enthusiastic reaction. However, he didn't say no. What he said to me was something that I have often thought back to, which I am sure sparked my entrepreneurial mindset. What he said was, "I will buy it for you, if you spend the weekend digging the vegetable garden."

Spending my whole weekend digging and sweating buckets over what was a massive vegetable garden would have made for a great end to the story; however, I also pointed out I was a lazy teenager. So, I decided not to do it. Miraculously, I could suddenly do without my once desperately needed Metallica box set.

It wasn't the right time for me to learn from his advice: you reap what you sow. Yet a few years later, all of those subtle hints and lessons were driven home when I met my uncle Bill in Perth, Australia. Seeing how my uncle had carved his dream life through hard work and determination finally hammered home my dad's words. When it comes to guidance or advice, it has got to be the right time for the recipient, and when it is, you need to be able to provide it. Sometimes, sadly, that will be after you have left this Earth.

I've hopefully already got you thinking about this subject with the previous questions, but here's some more:

If you could leave no money to your children, just a set of life principles, what would they be?

If you could live your life again, what if anything would you have done differently?

What advice would you give your future generations?

What did you learn during your life that you wish you'd grasped earlier?

This section of the book can be difficult, so in order to get those creative juices flowing, it is worth being a little more specific in your answers. For example, when people inherit money, for many it will be the first time they have had to deal with a significant lump of capital. The instinct is to buy a new car or a bigger house, or to simply leave it in the bank, so they don't decimate their inheritance. Your experience of owning this wealth tells you that investing some, most or all of that money wisely will probably be better in the long run. If not done before, sharing that advice now would be really sensible, otherwise the fruits of your labour may be lost all too quickly.

To help, here are some more questions to think through and answer, initially about money.

What principles have you learnt about money?

How would you *like* your Beneficiaries to use the money you've left to them?

How have you created your own financial success?

But life lessons don't just need to focus on money. When I am chatting to my daughters, I regularly tell them a joke they love. It goes something like this:

A worried looking 16-year-old girl is stood on a London street corner with a tattered violin case under her arm. A somewhat elderly gentleman in a long, grey trench coat approaches her, and says in his frail voice, "Can I help you miss?"

"Oh, thank you" the girl stammers nervously, "could you possibly tell me how I get to the Royal Concert Hall please?"

"Yes Miss, I can" he replies, "the best way to get to the Royal Concert Hall is through practice, practice, practice!"

Here are some more questions to help you think about what other lessons you could teach to your younger generations.

How would you suggest people live their lives?

From your experience in work and business, what advice would you give?

Outside of work, what have you learnt and what advice would you give?

What are the secrets to living a great life?

Knowing what you know now, what would you do differently if you were to start your career over?

How could you have achieved more in less time?

How should people prioritise their time?

Family, friendships, and our interactions with others in our community are fundamental parts of life, and our happiness, so guidance around these elements of our lives is incredibly valuable. In our Grandparents Interview, my mum's advice was to 'live the life that you want and to help others'. My mum's caveat to 'do what you want' was 'not when it was to the detriment of others'. It's sage advice and something that me, my sister and all of mum's grandchildren live by.

Here are some questions to help with this area of advice:

What is important to you about family and why?

What advice would you give to maximise your relationships?

I am a very goal orientated person. I set key goals to ensure I achieve what's important to me, but also to help me live the life that I think is best. For example, I set a 3-year goal to write my first book 'The Dream Retirement', with no experience in writing and no planned topics. But I hit that goal. I set another to complete an Ironman triathlon when I hadn't run or swam since school and managed to achieve that too. When living my life, I regularly ask myself, "will this action take me closer towards my end goal?" If I don't have the knowledge or skills to reach my goal initially, I make sure I take the needed steps to get there.

Here are some questions about goals and accomplishments:

What advice would you give about achievement?

How have you achieved your greatest successes?

Big, audacious achievements are wonderful, but often in life it's the little things that hold the most meaning and make the most impact. Grace, my wife's nanna, was known for making legendary Welsh Cakes. She made literally hundreds for our wedding, and they were all hoovered up by the guests before we came in from having our photos taken. Brenda, my mother-in-law, and Caryl, my wife, were sure to learn Grace's Welsh Cake skills while she was alive, so that this tradition could be passed on. Caryl still uses Grace's old spatula on St. David's Day to this day and the results are just as delicious.

Here are some questions to help you think about the little things:

What are the little things you'd want to pass on?

What are the things you've found that make people's lives better?

Are you known for any recipes, or something similar that you'd like to pass on?

What books would you recommend people read?

Values

In 1942, the U.S. merchant ship SS Alcoa Guide was attacked while carrying supplies from New Jersey to the Caribbean. During the night, a German submarine surfaced and opened fire on the ship. As the ship began descending to the ocean-floor, its crew managed to escape in two lifeboats and a raft. They had survived, but were far from safety, floating in the ocean hundreds of miles off the coast of North Carolina. Instead of sitting still and letting the currents of the sea take them where they may, the crew needed to make a plan. It started with the idea to navigate towards established shipping lanes. There, they'd hopefully be spotted by another ship or a plane from shore. The question was how to get there? The crew used a magnetic compass to make that decision. Like many explorers and navigators before them, the compass helped them point their boats in the right direction. A little over three days later, the two lifeboats were rescued.

Your best life won't spontaneously happen, so you can't leave it to chance. Living your best life takes deliberate action. Values will determine what shape your best life takes, but they won't just help you, they will also help those who come after you. So, we need to create your value compass.

I mentioned earlier in this chapter how important goals are to me. I actually split my life down into different roles, and then long term, 3-year, 1 year and quarterly goals for each area. Personally, I set goals for my family life, my health and wellbeing and my finances. Professionally, I set goals based on managing a business, being a Financial Planner and also being a marketeer. I even have amusing names for each, so instead of boring old 'Financial Planner', I call myself 'The Builder of Dreams!' Cheesy I know, but it certainly excites me more and gives me a clearer purpose.

For each one of my roles, I have found it to be incredibly powerful to determine what my values are. So, sticking with 'The Builder of Dreams', one of my values is to be empathetic. After more than 20 years in the industry, it is easy for me to think that I have seen it all, but to do a good job it is really important that I can empathise with my clients to ensure I get to the heart of their concerns. For my role as 'Super Dad and Husband', one of my values is to be a good listener; something that, as a typical bloke, I am always trying to improve upon!

You don't need to go as far as I take it, if you don't want to, so I'll give you a simpler approach. When faced with a tricky decision, I refer back to my values, so that my decision is in line with my core beliefs.

At Efficient Portfolio we spent a significant amount of time as a team working out what our values were. We questioned what it means to be part of Efficient Portfolio, what we stand for, and what we believe is important. The result, otherwise known as our values, spell out 'Efficient' and are:

Empathy   Helping people at a deeper level by really listening to their concerns.

Future Focused   Helping people make better decisions by looking into their financial future.

Financial Experts   Giving the best advice possible by achieving the highest qualifications.

Independent   Uncompromised advice, always.

Chartered   Achieving excellence and being at the top of our industry.

Innovative   Constantly looking to do things better for our clients.

Educational   Helping clients better understand their finances.

No Surprises   Nothing but open and honest advice.

Transparent   No smoke and mirrors so the client always knows what they are paying for.

As a team, when one of us is faced with a difficult decision, it is these values that we refer back to.

By documenting what your values are allows others to learn from your own life lessons in a slightly different way. Your core values are the beliefs you hold about what is most important in your life, and others can learn from that. Determining your values is often challenging, so give yourself some time to think about this. Write a list of the times when you were happiest, proudest, or most satisfied. Now, with those times in mind, look at the following table, and pick out the ten words that most resonate with you.

Acceptance	Cooperation	Fun	Moderation	Simplicity
Accomplishment	Courage	Generosity	Motivation	Sincerity
Accountability	Courtesy	Genius	Openness	Skilfulness
Accuracy	Creation	Giving	Optimism	Smart
Achievement	Creativity	Goodness	Order	Solitude
Adaptability	Credibility	Grace	Organisation	Spirit
Alertness	Curiosity	Gratitude	Originality	Spirituality
Altruism	Decisive	Greatness	Passion	Spontaneous
Ambition	Decisiveness	Growth	Patience	Stability
Amusement	Dedication	Happiness	Peace	Status
Assertiveness	Dependability	Hard work	Performance	Stewardship
Attentive	Determination	Harmony	Persistence	Strength
Awareness	Development	Health	Playfulness	Structure
Balance	Devotion	Honesty	Poise	Success
Beauty	Dignity	Honour	Potential	Support
Boldness	Discipline	Hope	Power	Surprise
Bravery	Discovery	Humility	Present	Sustainability
Brilliance	Drive	Humour	Productivity	Talent
Calm	Effectiveness	Imagination	Professionalism	Teamwork
Candour	Efficiency	Improvement	Prosperity	Temperance
Capable	Empathy	Independence	Purpose	Thankful
Careful	Empower	Individuality	Quality	Thorough
Certainty	Endurance	Innovation	Realistic	Thoughtful
Challenge	Energy	Inquisitive	Reason	Timeliness
Charity	Enjoyment	Insightful	Recognition	Tolerance
Cleanliness	Enthusiasm	Inspiring	Recreation	Toughness
Clear	Equality	Integrity	Reflective	Traditional
Clever	Ethical	Intelligence	Respect	Tranquillity
Comfort	Excellence	Intensity	Responsibility	Transparency
Commitment	Experience	Intuitive	Restraint	Trust
Common sense	Exploration	Joy	Results-oriented	Trustworthy
Communication	Expressive	Justice	Reverence	Truth
Community	Fairness	Kindness	Rigor	Understanding
Compassion	Family	Knowledge	Risk	Uniqueness
Competence	Famous	Lawful	Satisfaction	Unity
Concentration	Fearless	Leadership	Security	Victory
Confidence	Feelings	Learning	Self-reliance	Vigour
Connection	Ferocious	Liberty	Selfless	Vision
Consciousness	Fidelity	Logic	Sensitivity	Vitality
Consistency	Focus	Love	Serenity	Wealth
Contentment	Foresight	Loyalty	Service	Welcoming
Contribution	Fortitude	Mastery	Sharing	Winning
Control	Freedom	Maturity	Significance	Wisdom
Conviction	Friendship	Meaning	Silence	Wonder

Now you have your ten words, you need to prioritise them. Once done, drop the bottom three, as that way you'll have a list of your most important values. Once you have done that, I suggest that you write a paragraph about each of these values: why they are important, and why you have, or should have lived your life by them. There is a table set out in **The Life Legacy Planner** that can help you document these. To someone else,

106

this could prove to be the most important thing you put into that document.

Life Lessons

I mentioned in the last section that one of my roles in life is to be the best business owner I can be. I see this as even more important than being a Financial Planner. Too many small business owners spend their time being the best Financial Planner, accountant, or carpenter, and they fail to realise that their primary role is actually to run a good business.

In my efforts to be the best business owner I can be, I have attended The Strategic Coach Programme since around 2007. I have learnt a huge amount, but one of the most standout lessons is something that Dan Sullivan, the founder of Strategic Coach, calls 'The 4 Promises'. They are as follows:

1. Show up on time.
2. Do what you say.
3. Finish what you start.
4. Say please and thank you.

These simple rules are, to use their words, "the water that we human 'fish' swim in". They are fantastic principles to run your business by, and they have stood me in good stead since hearing them. Punctuality has always been vitality important to me; clearly a life lesson that was bestowed on me by my parents, so that has always been easy, but the others I probably had to be told to realise how powerful they are.

Over your life you will have come to realise that there are lessons you've learned that you'll never forget. Some will be deep and meaningful, and others less so.

When it came to the birth of mine and Caryl's second child, much of the childbirth experience was still new to us because

Ffion was born by emergency c-section. The birth didn't go according to plan, and whilst I will spare you the detail, it was more drawn out than it should have been.

After a long labour and difficult birth, I started to feel a little queasy. I've never been great with blood and gore, which is ridiculous as a farmer's son! As a result of how I was feeling, I took a seat next to Caryl, away from the 'business end', which meant that when our second born did finally arrive, I saw baby's entrance into the world through the arch of Caryl's legs.

I have to admit that the next few minutes remain a little blurry, but I definitely remember passing up the opportunity to cut the umbilical cord; that would have been the straw that broke the camel's back! But what I do remember is the midwife asking me to tell Caryl whether we had a boy or a girl. Of this I was certain, I had seen the evidence.

"We have a boy, a beautiful baby boy," I proclaimed. Prepared for most eventualities, we announced him to the world as Euan. He was wrapped up and passed to Caryl for her first cuddle. How perfect, a little baby brother to Ffion. The next steps were obvious. I called my parents and told them of our happy news.

After about 20 minutes, the midwife came back into the room, and asked if she could weigh baby Euan. "What a lovely name", she remarked as she up wrapped him up to put him onto the scales. At which point, she let out a small scream. What had happened, what was wrong? As a new parent it is moments like this that seem to last a lifetime. Was there a problem with his breathing? Had the midwife somehow hurt him? Or could it be something else even more worrying? These thoughts flash through your mind at 100 mph.

"I am afraid," she said, "that you do not have a baby boy at all. You do in fact have a beautiful baby girl."

"What? How? But I saw…." After 11 years the memories have faded a little, but what I thought I had 100% seen with my own eyes was in fact completely false. Obviously, I knew that there would be an umbilical cord, but I know what I saw, and it was the evidence required to sign off our new baby as a boy. And yet, what I saw, didn't actually exist. It was never there.

Fortunately, Bronwyn, as she was named after a fleeting 20-minute spell as Euan, was born early in the morning. As a result, I got straight back on the phone to my mum to correct my small, but important error. It actually was incredibly fortunate that Bronwyn was born early in the morning, as otherwise it would have probably taken about 3 hours to get through to Mum on the phone, by which time most of the East Midlands would have known we had been blessed with a baby boy.

The important point here is that our eyes often deceive us. I've learned through that sometimes we are adamant we have seen something, and yet we haven't. Our brain, our eyes and our memory can play tricks on us. Sometimes, even when we are certain about something, we can at a later stage be proved completely wrong.

That is one of my life lessons. A few others of mine, some small and some bigger that you can use for inspiration, are:

- Don't die wondering; give it a shot.
- Delegate, so that you can focus on your element.
- Set and repeatedly revisit clear goals for your life's roles.
- What other people think of me is none of my business.
- Bring energy and positivity to every situation.
- Ask daily, 'what's the best thing that has happened today' and 'what are you grateful for?'
- Meditate, read and journal daily.
- Any decision is better than no decision.

- Use a photo of a loved one as a bookmark.
- You are the average of the people you hang out with, so make wise choices.
- If you want to become wealthy beyond your dreams, read a book a week.
- Only talk to yourself as you'd talk to a friend.
- Make sure there is always a charge on the electric car (or fuel in the tank); you never know where you'll need to go without notice.
- Get up early and exercise.
- Always have some something creative on the go.
- Progress not perfection.
- Create more than you consume.
- The best inheritance you can leave your children is an education.
- If you think education is expensive, try ignorance. Invest in yourself.

Alternatively, here are Jordan Peterson's suggestions from his excellent book '12 Rules for Life'. You'll need to read the book though to make sense of some of them!

Rule 1: Stand up straight with your shoulders back.
Rule 2: Treat yourself like someone you are responsible for helping.
Rule 3: Make friends with people who want the best for you.
Rule 4: Compare yourself to who you were yesterday, not who someone else is today.
Rule 5: Do not let your children do anything that makes you dislike them.
Rule 6: Set your house in perfect order before you criticise the world.
Rule 7: Pursue what is meaningful (not what is expedient).
Rule 8: Tell the truth, or at least don't lie.

Rule 9: Assume that the person you are listening to might know something you don't.

Rule 10: Be precise in your speech.

Rule 11: Do not bother children when they are skateboarding.

Rule 12: Pet a cat when you encounter one on the street.

I am sure when you get started, you'll identify some incredible life lessons. There are loads of inspiring lists if you ask Google. This doesn't have to be perfect first time around; it can evolve, so just make a start now. Remember, progress not perfection!

Chapter 12: High Spirits

If you look up 'Spirit' in the dictionary it will tell you that it is 'the non-physical part of a person which is the seat of emotions and character; the soul.' But what constitutes your soul? What characteristics define who you truly are as a person?

Personally, I believe that your soul, or spirit, is made up of your heritage, wisdom, passion, and expertise, which all develop and evolve throughout your life. This chapter is all about how you can maximise these passions, impart your expertise so that others thrive in the future, and pass on your wisdom to your family, friends, and community- otherwise known as your 'tribe'.

Much of this chapter is about sharing your spirit with others and ensuring it lives on; but I will also look at what you can do whilst you are alive, as it is also important to nurture your soul by fulfilling your human needs, so you can live a happy life.

There are generally thought to be 6 human needs, but how do they relate to creating a legacy? There are 4 core human needs that must be achieved first, which are:

Certainty: We need to know that, for example, our wealth will be passed to the people we care most about. We also need to feel confident that we can comfortably enjoy the rest of our lives.

Variety: We need to experience a wide variety of activities, so we don't feel bored or that life is repetitive and monotonous.

Significance: We need to feel that we have a purpose and can make a difference to others through our own hard work and input.

| Connection: | Part of building our legacy is helping the people we love, and it feels rewarding and enjoyable to spend time with them, even more so when we can see with our own eyes the positive impact our legacy has. |

Assuming these 4 human needs are satisfied, in order to be truly happy you need to satisfy the final 2 human needs, which are:

| Growth: | We are happiest when we know the legacy we are leaving is actually growing rather than diminishing. On a personal level, age is not a reason to become stagnant or to stop learning, developing, or experiencing new things. |

| Contribution: | To feel truly fulfilled, we need to give back to our community, our family, or our friends. This could be through charity work, sharing our knowledge or simply 'helping out' to achieve a bigger goal. |

This chapter is very much about satisfying the human need of contribution. If you want to be truly happy for the rest of your life, you need to ensure that you are contributing to help others. And it doesn't need to be just about money!

The Family Tree

Retirement is a great opportunity to spend more time with your family. Research shows that it is both good for grandparents' longevity and also grandchildren's development if they spend more time together. No, this isn't me trying to wangle some free babysitting, honest! Spending more time as a family is good for everyone's wellbeing, so use this as an opportunity to think about how you could spend more quality time with the people you care most about. We can never be reminded of that too much.

Passing on your spirit to your family is arguably achieved in Chapter 10 with your 'legend'; however, there are ways to share more. I mentioned that 'heritage' is a fundamental part of your spirit, so one obvious way to pass this on is to build your family tree. I can't say I'd given a family tree much thought since my own school days, but that was until Bronwyn, my youngest daughter, was recently asked to compile one for her homework. The conversations we had around this showed us that already so much knowledge has been lost. As a family we can remember a couple of generations back, but not much more; the stories of these previous generations are incredibly difficult to track down.

I remember when I was a kid chatting to my dad's cousin Lilly. She was a tiny little lady that had the ferocity and energy of an army. Each year, in the lead up to Christmas, we paid her and her husband, Douglas, a visit. Douglas was no less of a character; I remember him queuing at the entrance to my cousin's wedding breakfast 3 times, just so that he could get multiple goes at kissing the bride!

On one visit, I remember Lilly telling me that she had been delving into her family tree and discovered that her family had links to the Russian Tsars. Whether this is true or not, I have no idea, and I haven't been able to verify her story, but wouldn't it be fascinating to know if that was the case? When I asked that side of the family about these incredible ancestors, they knew nothing of it. All that work that she did has potentially been lost, which is such a shame.

I've had even less success tracking down any interesting findings in my own family tree; the best I discovered was that my maternal great grandfather was an officer in the army. There was apparently an infamous story of him jumping the table in the Officers' Mess on horseback. Whilst this is more of an anecdotal story, the information we pass on doesn't always have to be outlandish or extravagant. What may seem normal to us today will not in the future, so the more we can record and save, the better future generations will be able to see into the lives of the people who have come before them.

As part of writing this book, and having been inspired by my youngest daughter's homework, I decided it was high time that I built our family tree so that the information wouldn't be lost for generations to come.

I used a few online resources to help with my project and whilst www.wikitree.com is better if you want to play genealogist and try to contact long lost relatives, my personal favourite is www.familyecho.com due to its simplicity. It's free, really easy to use and allows you to add photos and bios for each person. You can also easily print it or export it into other programs. The beauty of doing this digitally is that several people can add in what they know, so it can continue to evolve in the years to come, and as long as you keep a record of where it is in **The Life Legacy Planner**, it will never be lost!

My Family Tree

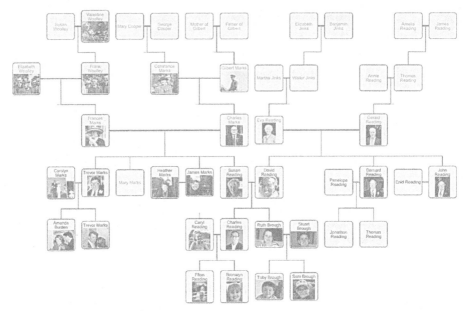

Community

The people who live in your community are often the people who benefit most from your contribution, especially as you get older. Whether it's the local sports club, the church, the school you attended or the village where you live, your community are often an incredibly important aspect of your life. The people in your community benefit from your time, your wisdom and often your money too! So, how will your spirit live on in that community? Now is the time to think about that. Is there anything you can do that will preserve your spirit within your community?

It could be a straightforward donation upon your death; it could be building something for that community in your name. Give some thought as to how you would like to be remembered in your community, and document it in **The Life Legacy Planner**, and if it's something that is really important to you, in your Will too.

As a wonderful example, at Oakham School, where I was educated to a greater or lesser extent, one former pupil donated money to allow the school to build the BAFS Pavilion, which is a wonderful new addition to the sports field that will be enjoyed by the students for generations to come. It doesn't have to be on such a grand scale as this though, it could be a bench in a local beauty spot that you are fond of visiting. To help collate your thoughts, you can use this template.

I would like to help my community in the following ways:

Community	Method	How much

Charity

Charity is a big thing for us at Efficient Portfolio. We give 1% of our time, profit, and expertise to charity each year, as well as taking every opportunity to raise money for our chosen cause. One charity particularly close to our hearts is the Motor Neurone Disease Association (MNDA) www.mndassociation.org, and we raised over £20,000 in 2018 for this vital cause through a gala dinner, a golf day, several of the team running their first marathon, and me completing my first Ironman. Over the years we've raised money for McMillan Cancer Support www.macmillan.org.uk, SPARKS Children's Charity www.gosh.org/about-us/sparks-charity and CALM (The Campaign Against Living Miserably) www.thecalmzone.net, to name a few.

Giving to charity is a wonderful way to give back after your success, to ensure your spirt and passion for something continues to thrive, but it's also a way to reduce Inheritance Tax too. I talked quite extensively about saving Inheritance Tax in Chapter 8, but it isn't all about shielding it from the tax man; it can also be achieved by doing good.

Gifts to charity upon your death are free of Inheritance Tax, so that means that your taxable estate is smaller, but of course that also means less money for your Beneficiaries. As I've mentioned though, the Government actively encourage people to leave some of their estates to charity and incentivise people by reducing IHT from 40% to 36% if you gift 10% or more of your estate to charity. That could be an existing charity, or a Charitable Trust that you have set up for a specific purpose. We've helped a few clients over the years set up such a Charitable Trust and it is a phenomenal way to leave a legacy. Imagine making some of your next generation Trustees of your own Charitable Trust, so that they can see the lasting impact and benefit that you have left behind? It wouldn't just be wonderful for them to see; it would also make a positive contribution to your community or the world in general.

So, give some thought as to how you could best help the world around you with your wealth. As a minimum, you should have an 'Ultimate Beneficiary' (the person or organisation who receives any residual funds left in the Trust when it reaches its maturity- usually around 125 years) in any Trusts you have, which will usually be a charity, so select one that you are passionate about. Over and above that, think about how your spirit could make a lasting difference to the areas of life that mean the most to you, and if it does involve a gift to a charity, make sure it is written into your Will.

Industry

I was recently chatting to a medical consultant who is a client of mine. He is at the top of his field, often called in as an expert witness in court cases, as well still running his own private practice. In a conversation about his future, he told me how much he loves the work he now does, because he is at the top position in his sector and solely focusses on what he truly loves about his work. And yet, he has the dilemma that whilst it has taken him 40+ years to get to this position, and he has become one of the best in the country at his specialism, he now feels that it is time to stop and retire.

The question of whether he should retire is one for another time, but it would be a travesty if his expertise and wisdom were lost from the medical world. I suggested that he could document what he'd learned, mentor a rising star or just carry on his work in a more advisory capacity. That way he could pass on more of what he has learned and ensure that his specialism continues to evolve. By doing these things, he would also be satisfying three of his human needs.

He would certainly be contributing to his profession, but he could also satisfy his need for growth, as it will likely mean he would still need to keep on top of the latest developments in his work. He would also experience significance, which is something people often lose after retiring from an important job. When anything satisfies three of your human needs, you are likely to become addicted to it, whether it be good or bad, and in this instance, it would be good.

I am passionate about being an entrepreneur and running my own business. I am always happy to give advice to people setting up their own businesses and have a future plan to create an incubator for new startups. When I speak at careers fairs, which I usually do once a year, I always end up talking as much about the difference between running a business and being employed in a business as I do about financial planning.

Whilst owning and running your own business isn't for everyone, it is in my opinion that it is the path that allows you the most freedom of what you do, and freedom of where, when and with whom you do it. If in the future I can create an incubator to help other small businesses with a place to base themselves, with access to advice and contacts, that that will be an amazing legacy to have created. I will certainly be passing on my spirit and passion for entrepreneurship, which will satisfy one of my human needs.

For now, I'll have to settle with my third book, 'Entrepreneurial Happiness', as my legacy in this area. If you want to download the first 3 chapters of this book for free, you can do so from www.efficientportfolio.co.uk/entrepreneurial-happiness

If you are not yet retired, or still have close ties with your former career, I'd recommend that you give some thought to the following questions:

How can I help my industry during my lifetime?

How can I help my industry after I am gone?

Hobbies

I love my hobbies. I love golf and I love competing in and training for triathlons. I am also a massive fan of the underwater world, and go scuba diving at every opportunity; well, every opportunity there is warm, clear water with interesting sea life! I'm not a huge fan of murky, cold water that contains the odd brown fish or disused shopping trolley! For me, scuba diving combines brilliantly with another of my passions, which is travelling. Travelling is so good for the soul, or mine at least:

seeing new places, experiencing new cultures, and meeting new people make up some of my fondest and most rewarding memories.

Writing this book got me thinking about how I could create a legacy in these areas. Golf is well supported, and other than a bench at my local club, I am not sure I need to add much value there. Triathlon on the other hand is expensive to get into, not financially rewarding for most people, and yet is such a fantastic and enriching experience, so I am considering setting up a Trust to help people enter into this sport after my passing.

With regards to travelling, as I said earlier in this book, I think I learnt more in 6 months travelling than I did in 3 years at university, so I am in the process of setting up a Trust that will allow my future generations to go travelling and to experience the world as I did. This essentially achieves what my grandad did for me, unbeknownst to him, by leaving me a small part of his legacy that I used to fund my travels. The Charlie Reading Travelling Trust will help future generations, and people connected to them, to experience the world when the time is right.

So how can you leave a legacy based on your hobbies? Give some thought to the following questions:

What hobbies am I passionate about?

How can I help others in these areas during my lifetime?

How can I help others in these areas after my passing?

Chapter 13: End with Today in Mind

It's ironic that a book about a future event finishes by talking about the present. I said right at the start of this book that our life is only given meaning by death. If we want to live the life we deserve, we have to appreciate today. We can't get too caught up in the future, although we need to live with an eye to it. We need to live for today.

Warm Hands

A client once said to me that "life is a bit arse about face". His words not mine! He said that "I had a beautiful wife who I loved and two wonderful children, both of whom I am enormously proud of. When my children were growing up, I had to spend most of my time working hard to ensure we had sufficient money to lead a comfortable life, so we rarely had the opportunity to enjoy time together."

He continued, "I am now at a stage in my life when I have lost my wife and both my children have families of their own and are hundreds of miles away. Physically, I am too frail to do many of the activities I loved. And yet I now have more money than I know what to do with, and few ways to enjoy it. Enjoy your life while you can."

His words really punched me in my heart. From that moment onwards, I decided that I wanted to help my children now so that they can enjoy the life they have now, as well as in the future. I want to be here to see them enjoy it.

Whilst you can leave a legacy upon your death, it is even better to leave one while you are still alive and can enjoy it. 'Giving with a warm hand' means that you can see your benefactors enjoy the fruits of your labour, and even enjoy those experiences together.

At my golf club, some of the older members refer to SKI holidays. SKI holidays don't always involve snow, because in this instance, SKI stands for 'Spend Kids' Inheritance.' I am all for this concept! You have worked hard for your wealth, and you should absolutely be enjoying it to the max. One of those ways can be with your family.

A few years ago, when my mum turned 70, she decided that her and Dad wanted to take the extended family on safari. My family plus my sister Ruth, with her husband and their two sons, Toby and Sam then aged 7 and 5, met up with Mum and Dad in Plettenberg Bay South Africa, where we enjoyed a wonderful few days doing everything from kayaking up Storms River to whale watching. We then jumped on a small plane and headed over to the Kwandwe Game Reserve. Kwandwe was an amazing place for a family safari, as being in the Cape it was free from Malaria and the team there were incredibly well geared up to deal with children of all ages.

Toby, Sam, Ffion, and Bronwyn had the most wonderful experience, seeing lions, elephants and even the elusive leopard in its natural habitat; an experience they talk about often to this day. Best of all, Mum and Dad were there to experience it with them. We all got to spend some amazing time together as a family. Now if that is a SKI holiday, I am all for it! It will certainly go down as one of the best holidays I have ever had, and to experience it as a family made it even more special.

I mentioned the 6 human needs that are required for happiness in the previous chapter. You will remember that 'contribution' is one of them, so the ironic thing about making gifts during your lifetime is that it is actually a way for you to become happier, i.e., by satisfying one of your own human needs. I also mentioned that if anything satisfies 3 or more of your human needs you are likely to become addicted to it because it feels so good. A SKI holiday with the family, whether it involves snow, sun or wildlife can certainly satisfy a need for contribution, for connection and for variety, so it is a brilliant way to create a legacy whilst also improving your own life.

Another example of making a contribution during your lifetime is by paying for a grandchild's education. One of my life lessons early on was that 'the best inheritance you can leave your children is an education'. I strongly believe this, as I was fortunate enough to receive a great education when I was growing up.

A great education is not just about the exam results either, it's about the life skills that are cultivated. Therefore, it doesn't have to be a private education; it could be travelling, music lessons or supporting someone financially whilst they are learning how to set up their own business. There are so many ways you can choose to create an education to give your loved ones an amazing start in life. It can be incredibly tax efficient for a grandparent to pay for things like a child's education too, particularly using Trusts like in Section 2, so this is another way to contribute to the legacy you leave.

To help, here are some questions to help you think about how you can contribute during your lifetime:

How can you start to create your legacy during your lifetime?

What do you wish you'd done in your life that you could help others do?

What was really important to you about your education, and how could you help others with that in mind?

To whom could 'giving with a warm hand' benefit now, as well as benefit you?

Goals

I've mentioned that I am big believer in setting goals, because I know that I achieve so much more as a result. If you want to leave the best legacy possible, you've got to achieve as much as possible during your life. Therefore, setting goals can help you to not only live a better life for yourself, but create a better life for those you leave behind.

At Efficient Portfolio, our mission statement is 'creating a better future through inspirational financial planning'. And we try and do that in every way we possibly can. One of the ways that we achieve this is by helping clarify our clients' goals and then helping them to achieve those specific, individual aims.

I believe that goals are incredibly powerful in pulling you forward and making your future even better than your present. At one of my Strategic Coach workshops, one of the fellow entrepreneurs in attendance announced that he had written book. I thought that was incredible and could instantly see how doing so differentiated him from his competitors, and how it established him as being the expert in his field. It completely inspired me, so at this workshop I set myself the goal of becoming a published author within 3 years. I had no idea how I was going to write a book though: I wasn't sure what the topic would be; I'm dyslexic; and have never been particularly good at writing!

But I did it and that book became 'The Dream Retirement', which was published in 2015. It took a lot of discipline to pull the book together, but I know that the real reason it came to fruition was because I wrote down my ultimate goal and broke it down into more manageable milestones.

Writing down clear end goals, even when you have no concept of how you're going to achieve something, is incredibly powerful. Clear end goals help you to pinpoint the smaller steps you need to take. This is a favourite adage of mine, which perfectly sums up how goals work: How do you eat an elephant? One bite at a time.

The starting point for me was firstly acknowledging what I wanted to achieve (i.e., to publish a book) and then asking myself what I had to do in the first year, in the first month and even the first day. I knew I needed to start the book by choosing my subject. Once I had that I could create a working title, begin my research and then look at publishing options. Developing this sequence helped me to roadmap what I wanted to achieve each month, week and day, so that the mountain I had to climb became a series of very small molehills.

Another example of this is when I had the genius idea of successfully completing an Ironman. Just in case you're not aware what an Ironman is, it consists of a two-and-a-half-mile swim, 112-mile bike ride, concluded with a 26.2-mile run. I appreciate that this type of goal is not everyone's cup of tea!

About 4 years ago, I was heavily into competitive cycling, but was looking for a new challenge. I read an inspirational book by Rich Roll, where he told his story about how he set out to complete 7 Ironman events in 7 days, on 7 different Hawaiian Islands. I won't ruin the ending for you, but it certainly lit a fire in my belly! Rich Roll's story sounded incredible, so I thought I wanted to give Ironman a go. I wasn't really sure that I was ever going to be serious about it, but I reasoned that I would never know unless I set myself the goal of trying.

So, a year or so after reading Rich Roll's book, I decided that if I was going to stand a chance of even finishing 1 Ironman, I better start by at least competing in 1 triathlon. That year I actually ended up completing a couple of sprint triathlons, an Olympic distance triathlon, and by the end of the year, I'd also done a half Ironman. This pattern continued into the next year and I added various triathlon feathers to my cap. I'm proud to say that by the summer of year 3, I crossed the finish line at Italy's Ironman and achieved my ultimate goal. Not bad for someone who didn't even know if they'd take it seriously in the first place!

I firmly believe that the only reason I succeed was because I set a clear goal and then worked backwards to create smaller steps. But more than that, I set SMART goals, i.e., Specific, Measurable, Attainable, Relevant, and Timely. This structure gave me an anchor for my focus and ensured that I made the best possible decisions that kept me on the right path.

Whilst SMART goals are important, I also think that goals should focus on 4 key areas of your life, namely health, wealth, relationships and your professional life, which can also include any voluntary or community work. By setting goals in these areas, you are likely to feel far more fulfilled and will satisfy your 6 human needs. In the table that follows, you can plot out your own goals. I encourage you to consider setting a goal for each of the 4 areas, look at what you have now to be able to achieve them, such as resources or skills, and consider what you need to acquire or do in order to achieve your aims.

One of the powers of setting goals is accountability and sharing them with other people gives you that. If other people know what your goals are, they will also be able to encourage and support you, or even expedite your progress. Who knows what opportunities will present themselves if you share your goals. You can find a template in **The Life Legacy Planner.**

The Bucket List

I don't know if you've seen the film 'The Bucket List' starring Jack Nicholson and Morgan Freeman, but I'd really encourage you to watch it. It's an incredibly funny yet moving film that's about ticking the off things that you must do before you 'kick the bucket'.

Whilst this section does cover the purpose of a Bucket List, it also centres around life's regrets. A couple of years ago I was at a conference in Miami, and I listened to a brilliant speaker called Ben Nemtin, whose talk was about what people's greatest regrets were at the end of their lives.

Almost echoing Bronnie Ware, Ben said that, whilst lying on their death beds, the top 5 regrets people had been:

1. That they wished that they'd lived a life that was true to themselves.
2. They wished they hadn't worked quite so hard.
3. They wished that they had let themselves be happier.
4. They wished they'd stayed better in touch with friends and family.
5. They wished they'd expressed their feelings more.

These are the sorts of things that are worth bearing in mind because we don't want to get to our death bed and have the same regrets.

In his talk, Ben told a story about what happened when he had just got to the end of his college education, and he started to experience some ill mental health, in the form of depression and anxiety. This was a low time for Ben, especially as he didn't know where life was going to take him. So, 3 of his friends banded together and said, "right, we're going to spend the summer trying to do something different."

What they decided to do was create an amazing Bucket List; a Bucket List of a hundred different things, which was latterly made into a TV series by MTV called 'The Buried Life'. That summer, they bought a big, purple bus and set off on the adventure of a lifetime.

The list they created wasn't the standard trip to Thailand or visit to the Taj Mahal; instead, the list was far more creative. As an example, one of the friends decreed that he would be a knight for the day.

Waking up one morning, the friend decided that today was the day! He hopped off the big, purple bus, decked out in full knightly regalia, and committed to spend the day acting just like a knight would. Suddenly, this kid spots 'the knight', runs up to him and kneels in front of him. Ben whispered in his friend's ear "You must now do what a knight would do."

The knight took his sword, tapped it on the boy's right shoulder then his left and declared that the boy was now a knight too. The boy got up beaming with happiness and suddenly another kid came up and he kneeled in front of Ben's friend. Before he knew it, he'd got a queue of kids lined up waiting to be knighted and a crowd appeared. Soon, the local media descended, subsequently ticking off another Bucket List item of being on the front page of a newspaper.

What the friends learnt was that by ticking off something on their own Bucket List, they also gave joy to other people. They also learnt that by talking about your Bucket List, and sharing it with other people, that's when the magic starts to happen.

Another item on Ben and his friends' Bucket List was that they wanted to play basketball with President Obama. They all thought it was a pretty outlandish and audacious goal, especially as they were in Canada and not even in the USA, but they still put it on their list.

To at least try and tick it off, Ben wrote to a Senator, who actually replied saying that he admired his enthusiasm, but it was a 'no'. So, Ben wrote to a different Senator, who was higher ranking in the White House. Again, the reply stated that the idea was great, but it was a 'no'. Not one to be so easily deterred, Ben put pen to paper for a third time, and a fourth time, and a fifth time, until eventually, he received a call asking "do you still want to come and play basketball at the White House? President Obama won't be here, but if you want play basketball on his court at the White House, will that do?"

After about two seconds of discussion, the friends all said "Yeah, that'll do!" So, off they went to Washington to play basketball on the White House's private courts. Once they got there, as you can imagine, they were beyond excited and were having the time of their lives, when of the friends exclaims "My God! Turn around."

Guess who walked onto the court? None other than President Obama, who then shot a few hoops with them. And he really did! In Ben's TED Talk, there's a photo of them standing on the court with Barack Obama:
www.youtube.com/watch?v=H6Y7mfxEaco

So, just how did this come to pass? The truth is it was because Ben and his friends were persistent and audacious. It was also because they shared their list. These are the key components to creating an amazing Bucket List and for those goals to become realities.

When I wrote 'The Dream Retirement', I also wrote my Bucket List, and it was about all the bigger things in life like trips abroad. After seeing Ben's talk, I revisited my Bucket List and added lots more small things that would just be fun. These ranged from sending a message in a bottle to playing football at the Nottingham City ground (yes, I am a Nottingham Forest fan!) The new list also included meaningful things like taking a homeless person out for lunch and saving somebody's life.

I shared my new list with my team at Efficient Portfolio and that's when the magic started to happen. One of our Financial Planners, Tom, told me that one of his clients holds an annual corporate day at the Forest grounds, and he would see if he could get me involved; another one of my team, Alex, then said, "oh, I could organise a lunch for you with a homeless person." That's the power of sharing.

I could talk for days about the Bucket List, but what I really want you to do is to create your own, which you can do using **The Life Legacy Planner**. Exciting things will happen when you do this, and share it, so please get in touch to tell me your stories, as I would love to hear them.

Message in a Bottle

Death is obviously a very delicate topic, laced with emotion. Sitting down and writing about it has brought up a whole host of feelings for me, and it has also reminded me of a touching poem that I once read.

The poem below was supposedly found in the possessions of a deceased Australian man in a care home; however, after more research it seems that it is a hybrid of a poem called 'Look Closer' or 'Crabbit', as it's otherwise known, by Scottish nurse Phyllis McCormack in 1966, and an adaptation of this poem called 'Cranky Old Man' by David L Griffith. The poem, whatever its source, is a poignant reminder of life and of old age, so I felt it was appropriate to share it with you.

Cranky Old Man
What do you see nurses? ......What do you see?
What are you thinking.... when you're looking at me?

A cranky old man ...not very wise,
Uncertain of habit ..... with faraway eyes?
Who dribbles his food ... and makes no reply.
When you say in a loud voice .'I do wish you'd try!'
Who seems not to notice ...the things that you do.
And forever is losing ... . A sock or shoe?
Who, resisting or not ... ... lets you do as you will,
With bathing and feeding ... .The long day to fill?
Is that what you're thinking? Is that what you see?
Then open your eyes, nurse .You're not looking at me.
I'll tell you who I am .... .. As I sit here so still,
As I do at your bidding, as I eat at your will.
I'm a small child of Ten. .with a father and mother,
Brothers and sisters .... who love one another
A young boy of Sixteen ... .. with wings on his feet
Dreaming that soon now ...... a lover he'll meet.
A groom soon at Twenty ... ..my heart gives a leap.
Remembering, the vows .. .. .that I promised to keep.
At Twenty-Five, now ... . .I have young of my own.
Who need me to guide ... And a secure happy home.
A man of Thirty . ... My young now grown fast,
Bound to each other .... With ties that should last.
At Forty, my young sons .. .have grown and are gone,
But my woman is beside me . . to see I don't mourn.
At Fifty, once more, ...Babies play 'round my knee,
Again, we know children ... . My loved one and me.
Dark days are upon me ... . My wife is now dead.
I look at the future ... . I shudder with dread.
For my young are all rearing ... young of their own.
And I think of the years ... And the love that I've known.
I'm now an old man ... . and nature is cruel.
It's jest to make old age ... . Look like a fool.
The body, it crumbles...... . Grace and vigour, depart.
There is now a stone ... where I once had a heart.

But inside this old carcass. A young man still dwells,
And now and again …. . my battered heart swells
I remember the joys …. .. . I remember the pain.
And I'm loving and living … …. Life over again.
I think of the years, all too few …. Gone too fast.
And accept the stark fact … that nothing can last.
So open your eyes, people …. . …. open and see.
Not a cranky old man.
Look closer …. See ……….. ME!!

If you believe the story in the poem, the 'cranky old man' chose to leave behind a poem that gave people an insight into what he was thinking. I am sure if his loved ones got to read it, it would have brought tears to their eyes. It certainly made me think of my own life, and whether I am making the most of it.

When you leave money to people in your Will, wouldn't it be better if it came with a message of why you left it to them, and how you hope they might use it? It might not be a poem, but a few short words could make a massive impact on how others enjoy your legacy and the life they lead.

Give the following questions some thought for each benefactor of your Will.

Why am I leaving this to you?

How would you like them to use it?

Any advice you'd give them about using it?

Chapter 14: The End is the Start

I hope that by reading this book you have been able to look at death in a slightly more positive light. I also hope that you have identified some new ways that you can create an amazing legacy for the people who you care most about, as well as pinpoint some ways that can make your life better too. It is my belief that if you complete the processes and exercises laid out in this book, you will improve each of those aspects of your life.

To quote Vinnie Jones from the legendary Guy Richie film 'Lock Stock and Two Smoking Barrels', I hope that "It's been emotional'. If it has, that means you are getting closer to what is really important to you, and the people you care most about.

To finish off this book, I wanted to give you a summary of the actions you should be taking to truly create your very own Life Legacy Gift. The best place to tick these off is on **The Life Legacy Planner** and, if you're a client of Efficient Portfolio, to save this in your client portal; however, ultimately it doesn't matter how you do it as long as a) it works for you; b) the people who need to know do; and c) they have access to it when they need it.

1. Put thought into the first 14 days after death and set out what's needed to ease the pain of those around you.
2. Set up ICE (in case of emergency) numbers in your mobile so that the right people can be contacted.
3. Think about who needs access to your property and how that would happen.

4. Document your funeral wishes so you actually get what you want.
5. Think about what medical treatment you do or don't want and what a good death for you would be, so you get the treatment you think is appropriate.
6. Document all your key information in one place so that it can be easily found.
7. Create a list of key financial assets, bank accounts and investments so nothing is missed.
8. Document all of your insurance, and make sure that if you are a couple, you are both listed on the home insurance, so that policies can be claimed on or cancelled.
9. Pass the baton by ensuring both parties in your relationship understand your finances sufficiently well to reduce their worry.
10. Document your liabilities to make probate quicker.
11. Keep all of your passwords in a centralised place and give those who need to the ability to access your accounts when the time is right, so you can reduce the work for your Executors.
12. Create a list of your utility providers and memberships to save Executors' time.
13. Create a Chattels List of your most important or valuable possessions, so nothing is overlooked.
14. Work out what should happen to your pets and document it, so that there is a plan.
15. Document anything you want created as a memorial to your life, so you are remembered more often.
16. Create a Key Document List, stating where each document is located so that the people that need to know do.
17. If you run your own business, consider the effect of a death on the employees, the business viability, the

fellow shareholders, and the families of all shareholders. Also create a Contingency Plan and perhaps a Business Will, so that the business can continue to live on without you.

18. Ensure you have a well written and up-to-date Will in place, so that what you want to happen does.

19. Make Lasting Powers of Attorney, so you can be looked after in accordance with your wishes.

20. Create a Trust Framework to ensure that your assets pass down through the bloodline in a tax efficient and protected manner.

21. Implement strategies to reduce Inheritance Tax, so that your family can inherit more of your hard work.

22. Document your story or legend, so that it is not forgotten. A book is an amazing way to do this and is easier than you think.

23. Video 'The Grandparent Interviews', so your future generations can see and hear from your life experiences.

24. Organise your photos so that your life memories can be accessed easily by future generations.

25. Document advice that you would give based on the life you've led, so that future generations can learn from your experience.

26. Write a list of your values and life lessons for others to learn from.

27. Create and share your family tree, so that future generations know where they came from.

28. Look at how you can help your community and the charities your care about, so that your spirit lives on.

29. Think about how you can create a legacy based on your hobbies or industry during your lifetime and after you are gone.

30. Create goals and a Bucket List, so that you live the life you deserve.
31. Think about making gifts with warm hands instead of after you have gone, so that you can witness their effect.
32. Consider a SKI (Spend Kids Inheritance) holiday, or other ways so that you can create a legacy with your family during your lifetime.
33. Leave messages with the gifts, so that you can tell the recipient why you've done it and how you'd ideally like them to use it.

This may well seem like a long list but remember that it's all about progress not perfection. Something is always better than nothing, so just make a start. Each step is another chapter in your own Life Legacy Gift.

At Efficient Portfolio, if we can help you with any of the steps towards creating your legacy, we'd be honoured to help. As a client, you can always contact your Client Relationship Manager or your Financial Planner to help you with these. If you aren't a client, you can always contact us at hello@efficientportfolio.co.uk or on 01572 898060. You can also find out much more about us and hear some of our 'Client Stories' at www.efficientportfolio.co.uk.

The idea of putting this into both a book and **The Life Legacy Planner** is to try and bring together the convenience of reading a book and the practicalities of building a digital life legacy. I hope it has helped you achieve that. If you know someone else who you think would benefit from reading this book, please contact us as we'd be more than happy to send them a copy. After all, the more people who build their Life Legacy Gift, the better everyone's legacies will be.

As a penultimate thought, remember that if you do the same today as you did yesterday, you'll get the same results as you got today, so take some action to implement your very own Life Legacy Gift. You will be making a bigger impact on your future generations than you can possibly imagine.

I will finish this book with one final thought. If death gives life meaning, then the goal is not to live forever, but instead to create something else that does. So, get on and build your Life Legacy Gift, and you will have created something immortal.

Bibliography and Links

To download your Life Legacy Gift Planner, please visit:
www.efficientportfolio.co.uk/life-legacy-gift

The Death Notification Service:
www.deathnotificationservice.co.uk

'33 Meditations on Death: Notes from the Wrong End of Medicine' by David Jarret, Transworld Digital (16 April 2020)

NHS Organ Donation: www.organdonation.nhs.uk

Advance Statements: www.nhs.uk/conditions/end-of-life-care/advance-statement

Free download of 'SMART Money: How to Create Financial Freedom': www.efficientportfolio.co.uk/smart

Dashlane: www.dashlane.com

Roboform: www.roboform.com

How to Password Protect a Document (Microsoft):
https://support.microsoft.com/en-us/office/protect-a-document-with-a-password-05084cc3-300d-4c1a-8416-38d3e37d6826?ui=en-us&rs=en-us&ad=us

Cremation Sculptures: www.castingashes.com

Purchase and Name a Star: www.starregistry.ca

Living Reef Memorial: www.livingreefmemorial.com

Memory Bear: www.hiddentreasurecrafts.com/how-to-make-a-memory-bear

Efficient Portfolio Website: www.efficientportfolio.co.uk

Efficient Portfolio Email: hello@efficientportfolio.co.uk

Lifetime Cash-Flow Forecasting: www.efficientportfolio.co.uk/what-is-lifetime-cashflow-forecasting

Life Legacy Roadmap: www.efficientportfolio.co.uk/life-legacy-roadmap-course

The 2 Minute Retirement Plan: www.efficientportfolio.co.uk/tools/the-2-minute-retirement-plan

The 1 Minute Wealth Protector: www.efficientportfolio.co.uk/tools/the-1-minute-wealth-protector

Dictionary References: www.languages.oup.com/google-dictionary-en

Book Mapping Tool: www.miro.com

Online Transcription: www.Rev.com

Online Video Storage and Publication Platforms: www.Youtube.com , www.Vimeo.com or www.Wistia.com

The Grandparent Interviews: www.efficientportfolio.co.uk/life-legacy-gift

The Dream Retirement: www.dream-retirement.com

Photograph Scanning: www.filmscanuk.co.uk

Online Photo Book Builders: www.bobbooks.co.uk and www.snapfish.co.uk and www.myphotographics.co.uk.

Online Document and File Storage: www.dropbox.com, www.icloud.com and www.google.com/drive

'The Top Five Regrets of the Dying: A Life Transformed by the Dearly Departing', by Bronnie Ware, Hay House UK (13 Aug. 2019)

Story about the SS Alcoa Guide:
www.mindfulambition.net/values

'12 Rules for Life: An Antidote to Chaos' by Jordan Peterson, Penguin; 1st edition (2 May 2019)

Ancestry Resources: www.wikitree.com and www.familyecho.com

Motor Neurone Disease Association (MNDA):
www.mndassociation.org

McMillan Cancer Support: www.macmillan.org.uk

 SPARKS Children's Charity: www.gosh.org/about-us/sparks-charity

CALM (The Campaign Against Living Miserably:
www.thecalmzone.net

First 3 Chapters of Entrepreneurial Happiness:
www.efficientportfolio.co.uk/entrepreneurial-happiness

'Finding Ultra' by Rich Roll, Three Rivers Press; Reprint edition (31 May 2013)

'The Bucket List', Directed and Produced by Rob Reiner, Written by Justin Zackham. Warner Brother Studios, 2007.

'The Buried Life', MTV, 2010

Ben Nemtin Ted Talk:
www.youtube.com/watch?v=H6Y7mfxEaco

'Look Closer' or 'Crabbit', by Phyllis McCormack ,1966

'Cranky Old Man' by David L Griffith.

'Lock Stock and Two Smoking Barrels', Directed by Guy Richie, PolyGram Filmed Entertainment, 1998

Printed in Great Britain
by Amazon